30秒でできる！
ニッポンの歴史紹介
おもてなしの英会話

安河内哲也＝監修

IBC PUBLISHING

本書の音声ダウンロードは
弊社ホームページから！

www.ibcpub.co.jp/shokai/

装　　幀＝斉藤 啓（ブッダプロダクションズ）
編集協力＝James M. Vardaman
　　　　　賀川 真

はじめに

　本書は、刊行してから大好評を博している『30秒でできる！ニッポン紹介　おもてなしの英会話』の姉妹版です。日本を訪れた外国人たちは、神社仏閣や城などを観光し、温泉に浸かって一息ついて、杯を傾けながら和食に舌鼓を打つ……というのが定番なのですが、その外国人のみなさんが１日を振り返りながら興味を抱くのが「ニッポンの歴史」なのです。

　たとえば、外国の人たちを皇居に案内していたら、「なぜ、将軍は戦うことなく江戸城を明け渡したのですか？」などと質問を受けたりしてしまいます。自分の国の歴史だからある程度は分かっているつもりかもしれませんが、いざ英語で答えようとすると、なかなか言葉がでてこない、ということがよくあるのです。ふだんの会話では使わない単語が、歴史を説明するときには必要になってくるからです。例えば「薩摩藩」のことを"Satsuma clan"というとか、「江戸幕府」は"Tokugawa shogunate"などです。

　本書では、外国人によく聞かれる日本の歴史について、古代から現代まで時代を追いながらカバーしました。それも、簡単に短く、１トピックのうち１つの質問につき30秒で、日本の歴史を説明するための英語が収録されています。

　もちろん、日本史の解釈にはさまざまなものがあります。本書で記されている解釈は１つの視点であるに過ぎません。読者のみなさんの考えや解釈が、そこに付加され外国の方に伝われば、より生き生きとした交流が促進されるはずです。

　本書を通し、より深い異文化交流を進めていただければ幸いです。

目次

はじめに　3

第1章　日本史の概要
Outline of Japanese History

1. 日本の歴史の長さ 10
2. 日本の史跡 12
3. 日本の外交 14
4. 日本の戦争 16
5. 武士と侍の違いとは？ 18
6. 将軍と幕府 20
7. 大名 22
8. 忍者 24
9. 大奥 26
10. 舞妓 28
11. 城 30

第2章　日本の伝統文化の歴史
History of Japanese Traditional Culture

1. 日本の演劇 34
2. 日本の生活文化 36
3. 日本の伝統スポーツ 38
4. 日本の古典文学 40
5. 日本の古典絵画 42
6. 日本の宗教 44

第3章　日本の古代
Ancient Japan

1. 先史時代 48
2. 先史時代の国際交流 50

Contents

- 3　大和朝廷の成立 ... 52
- 4　飛鳥時代 ... 54
- 5　大化の改新 ... 56
- 6　律令制度 ... 58

第4章　奈良時代
Nara Period

- 1　平城京 ... 62
- 2　遣唐使 ... 64
- 3　日本正史の誕生 ... 66

第5章　平安時代
Heian Period

- 1　平安京 ... 70
- 2　藤原氏 ... 72
- 3　平安文学 ... 74
- 4　平安仏教 ... 76
- 5　武士の台頭 ... 78
- 6　平安時代の武装勢力 ... 80
- 7　院政と保元・平治の乱 ... 82
- 8　平家の繁栄と滅亡 ... 84

第6章　鎌倉時代
Kamakura Period

- 1　源氏と北条氏 ... 88
- 2　承久の乱 ... 90
- 3　元寇 ... 92
- 4　鎌倉文学 ... 94
- 5　鎌倉仏教 ... 96
- 6　鎌倉幕府の崩壊と建武の新政 ... 98

第7章 室町時代
Muromachi Period

1. 室町幕府と南北朝 102
2. 北山文化 104
3. 倭寇と応仁の乱 106
4. 東山文化 108
5. 戦国時代 110
6. 戦国大名 その1 112
7. 戦国大名 その2 114
8. 西洋との出会い 116

第8章 安土桃山時代
Azuchi Momoyama Period

1. 戦国時代の終了 120
2. 織田信長 122
3. 豊臣秀吉 124
4. 秀吉の政策 126
5. 朝鮮出兵 128
6. 関ヶ原の戦い 130
7. 安土桃山文化 132

第9章 江戸時代
Edo Period

1. 江戸時代の始まり 136
2. 徳川家康 138
3. キリスト教の禁止 140
4. 鎖国 142
5. 大名と幕府 144
6. 身分制度と農本経済 146
7. 元禄文化 148
8. 江戸時代の経済 150

Contents

- 9 江戸時代の社会問題 152
- 10 化政文化 154
- 11 開国 156
- 12 尊王攘夷 158
- 13 幕末の情勢 160
- 14 江戸幕府の滅亡 162

第10章 明治時代
Meiji Period

- 1 明治維新 166
- 2 明治最初の政策 168
- 3 文明開化 170
- 4 自由民権運動と憲法制定 172
- 5 日清戦争 174
- 6 日露戦争 176
- 7 明治時代の文化 178

第11章 大正時代
Taisho Period

- 1 大正時代の概要 182
- 2 大正時代の政治 184
- 3 関東大震災 186
- 4 大正時代の文化 188

第12章 昭和──戦前
Showa Period: Prewar

- 1 大正から昭和へ 192
- 2 世界恐慌 194
- 3 自由な社会の終焉 196
- 4 日中戦争の開始 198
- 5 日中戦争時の政策 200

	6	第二次世界大戦へ......202
	7	敗戦に向けて......204

第13章 昭和――戦後
Showa Period: Postwar

1	日本の占領......208
2	日本の民主化......210
3	冷戦と日本の主権回復......212
4	高度経済成長......214

第14章 戦後から現代へ
Postwar Japan to the Present

1	日本文化の輸出......218
2	憲法改正......220
3	靖国神社問題......222
4	食料自給率......224
5	老舗......226
6	人口高齢化......228
7	変わりゆく日本の男性像と女性像......230

第1章
Chapter 1

日本史の概要

Outline of Japanese History

1 日本の歴史の長さ

❓ こんな質問をされたら？

1 How long have people lived in Japan?
日本にはいつごろから人が住んでいましたか？

2 How long is the history of Japan?
日本の歴史はどのくらいの長さですか？

3 How long ago did the Emperors begin?
日本の天皇はどのくらい前からいるのですか？

日本列島

The Length of Japanese History

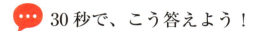 30秒で、こう答えよう！

1. In the Paleolithic period, what is now Japan was attached to the Asian continent. A hundred thousand years ago, people from the continent had already migrated to Japan. Other immigrants coming from the islands of the Pacific Ocean are believed to have reached Japan as well.

   旧石器時代、現在の日本はアジア大陸にくっついていました。数十万年前、すでに大陸から日本へ移住した人たちがいました。他にも太平洋の島々からの移住者が日本に到達したと信じられています。

2. Japanese history can be traced back to almost 2,000 years ago.

   日本史は、ほぼ2000年遡ることができます。

3. Legends say that Emperor Jinmu became the first emperor in 660, but there are no historical records to prove it.

   伝説によれば、神武天皇は紀元前660年に最初の天皇となったとされますが、これを証明する歴史的な記録は存在しません。

2 日本の史跡

❓ こんな質問をされたら？

1 Where are many of Japan's historical landmarks?

日本の史跡の多い場所はどこですか？

2 Where are historical landmarks near Tokyo?

東京近郊の史跡はどこにありますか？

3 Where is a museum where one can learn about Japanese history?

日本の歴史がわかる博物館を教えてください。

東京国立博物館

Japan's Historical Landmarks

 30秒で、こう答えよう！

1. Because it was the capital city for such a long time, it is natural that most of the country's historical landmarks are concentrated in Kyoto.

   やはり長い間首都だった京都に多くの史跡が集中しています。

2. In Kamakura, Kanagawa Prefecture, which was the seat of the Kamakura Bakufu, the whole city projects the atmosphere of a historical landmark.

   鎌倉幕府のあった神奈川県鎌倉市は、街全体が史跡のムードを漂わせています。

3. There are various historical museums throughout the country, but in terms of scale and content, the most substantial are the national museums. There are national museums in Tokyo, Kyoto, Nara, and Dazaifu, in Fukuoka Prefecture.

   日本各地にさまざまな歴史博物館がありますが、規模、内容ともに最も充実しているのは国立博物館です。国立博物館は東京のほか、京都、奈良、福岡県太宰府市にあります。

3 日本の外交

❓ こんな質問をされたら？

1 Which countries did ancient Japan have relations with?

古代の日本はどんな国と付き合っていましたか？

2 When did Japan begin to have relations with Western countries?

日本はいつごろから西洋人と付き合い始めましたか？

3 How long did Japan's period of seclusion last?

日本はどのくらいの期間、鎖国をしていましたか？

鎖国時代の長崎の出島

Japan's International Relations

 30秒で、こう答えよう！

1 In the ancient era, Japan had relations with the Korean Peninsula and China.

古代の日本は、朝鮮半島や中国と国交を持っていました。

2 Around the fifteenth century, Japanese people encountered Europeans.

15世紀頃、日本人はヨーロッパ人と遭遇しました。

3 Japan was secluded from the world between 1641 and 1853.

日本は1641年から1853年の間、世界から遮断されていました。

4 日本の戦争

? こんな質問をされたら？

1 Was Japan ever attacked by a foreign country?

日本は外国から攻められたことがありますか？

2 Did Japan ever attack a foreign country?

日本が外国を攻めたことはありますか？

3 Was Japan ever occupied by a foreign country?

日本が外国に占領されたことはありますか？

原爆によるキノコ雲

Japan's Wars

第1章 日本史の概要

 30秒で、こう答えよう！

1 Japan has only been attacked twice. The first time was the invasion by the Mongolian Empire in the thirteenth century, and the second was World War II.

日本はわずかに2度、攻撃を受けました。最初は13世紀のモンゴル帝国による侵入で、2回目が第二次世界大戦でした。

2 Toyotomi Hideyoshi declared war against the Ming Dynasty of China and invaded Korea. The Sino-Japanese war broke out in 1894. The Russo-Japanese war broke out in 1903.

豊臣秀吉は中国の明朝に宣戦布告し、朝鮮を侵略しました。日清戦争は1894年に起こりました。日露戦争が1903年に勃発しました。

3 Japan lost the Pacific War in 1945 and was occupied by allied nations led by the United States.

日本は1945年に太平洋戦争に敗れ、アメリカが率いる連合国に占領されました。

5 武士と侍の違いとは？

? こんな質問をされたら？

1 Who were the samurai?

侍とはどういう人達のことですか？

2 How did the samurai live?

侍はどういう生活をしていましたか？

3 What is the difference between samurai and *bushi*?

侍と武士はどう違うのですか？

侍

The Samurai?

 30秒で、こう答えよう！

1 In many respects, the samurai were like knights and had to undergo rigorous training to serve their masters or lords.

多くの点で、侍は騎士のようなものでした。君主に仕えるために厳格な訓練を行わなければなりませんでした。

2 Samurai had to undergo rigorous training, and study philosophy and ethics to achieve a level of refinement.

侍は厳格な訓練を行い、ある水準の教養を身につけるために哲学や道徳を学ばなければなりませんでした。

3 Samurai were also called *bushi*. *Bushi* means "warrior," while samurai literally means "person who serves."

侍は武士とも呼ばれました。武士とは「戦士」を意味します。一方、侍 は「仕える人」を意味します。

6 将軍と幕府

❓ こんな質問をされたら？

1 What did the shogun do?

将軍とはどういうものですか？

2 What was the Shogunate (*Bakufu*)?

幕府とはどういうものですか？

3 How long did the Shogunate last?

幕府はどのくらいの期間ありましたか？

徳川家初代将軍　徳川家康

Shogun and Bakufu

💬 30秒で、こう答えよう！

1 Originally, the shogun was just a military general appointed by the emperor. Over time, the position of shogun became just like that of a king.

元来、将軍は天皇によって任命された単なる軍の大将でした。時間が経つにつれて、将軍の地位は王様のようなものになりました。

2 In the feudal period, the shogun and his government made almost all executive decisions for the nation.

封建時代、将軍と幕府が国のためにほとんど全ての行政上の決断を行いました。

3 The shogunate system was started by Minamoto no Yoritomo in 1192. When the Tokugawa Shogunate Government was overthrown in 1868, the era of the samurai also ended.

幕藩体制は1192年に源頼朝によって始められました。徳川幕府が1868年に転覆されたとき、侍の時代もまた終焉を迎えたのです。

7 大名

❓ こんな質問をされたら？

1 What did the feudal lords do?
大名とはどういう人達のことですか？

2 Did the feudal lords fight against each other?
大名同士に争いはありましたか？

3 When did the feudal lords stop fighting?
大名同士の争いはいつ終わりましたか？

豊臣秀吉

Daimyo, Feudal Lords

 30秒で、こう答えよう！

1 A daimyo was a lord who had his own domain and served the shogun.

大名とは領国を持ち将軍に仕える君主のことでした。

2 In the Warring States period, between 1467 and 1573, daimyo became powerful, and they fought each other to take control of their regions.

1467年から1573年までの戦国時代、大名が台頭し、互いの領地を巡って争いました。

3 When Toyotomi Hideyoshi united Japan again in 1590, all daimyo became obedient to the new government.

豊臣秀吉が1590年に再び日本を統治したとき、全ての大名が新政権に従いました。

8 忍者

❓ こんな質問をされたら？

1 What kind of people were ninja?

忍者とはどういう人ですか？

2 Were some ninja women?

女性の忍者もいたのですか？

3 What area had lots of ninja?

忍者の多い場所はどこですか？

忍者　北斎画

Ninja

💬 **30秒で、こう答えよう！**

1 These were groups of spies that appeared during the Warring States Period. Most of these groups had no direct lord-vassal relationship with a particular daimyo and were instead hired as mercenary soldiers.

戦国時代頃に現れたスパイ集団です。大名と直接の主従関係を持たず、傭兵として雇われるケースがほとんどでした。

2 There are records of female ninja, called *kunoichi*, from the period of the daimyo Takeda Shingen.

いわゆる「くノ一」が女性の忍者で武田信玄の頃から記録があります。

3 Three famous ninja villages were Iga (Mie Prefecture), Koga (Shiga Prefecture), and Yagyu (Nara Prefecture).

有名な忍者の里は三重県伊賀、滋賀県甲賀、奈良県柳生などです。

9 大奥

? こんな質問をされたら？

1 What kind of place was the *Ooku*?

大奥とはどのようなところですか？

2 When did the *Ooku* start?

大奥はいつ始まりましたか？

3 Who was the most powerful person in the *Ooku*?

大奥の最高権力者は誰ですか？

千代田之大奥　歌合　橋本

The Ooku, Great Interior of Edo Castle

 30秒で、こう答えよう！

1 It was the inner palace building which was the residence of the sovereign's lawful wife and various concubines, together with the female government officials who tended to the affairs of the legitimate wife.

君主の正室や側室、さらには君主や正室の私生活の世話をする女性の官僚などが生活をしていた日本の後宮です。

2 It did not become formalized until the Edo Period when Kasuga no Tsubone (1579–1643), the former nursemaid to the third Edo shogun, Tokugawa Iemitsu, established it.

大奥を組織的に整備したのは江戸幕府三代将軍家光の乳母春日局によるものとされています。

3 The shogun's legitimate wife was referred to as the overall director of financial affairs, but in fact the shogun's birth mother or the concubine who bore the shogun's eldest son often held the real power.

一応将軍の正室が「御台所」と呼ばれる総取締役ですが、将軍の生母や嫡男を生んだ側室などが実際の力を持っていました。

10 舞妓

? こんな質問をされたら？

1 What kind of people are *maiko*?

舞妓とはどういう人達ですか？

2 Are *maiko* different from *oiran*?

舞妓と花魁は違うのですか？

3 Where can one find *maiko*?

舞妓さんはどこにいますか？

舞妓

Maiko

 30秒で、こう答えよう！

1. In Japan, these are particularly young women who sing and dance to entertain guests in traditional eating and drinking establishments. Wearing white makeup and dressed in kimono, they are well versed in the arts.

   日本の伝統的な飲食店で歌や踊りで客をもてなす女性のなかでも若手の女性ことです。顔に白粉を塗り、着物姿で、様々な芸事に精通しています。

2. They are completely different. The *oiran* were licensed prostitutes who existed until the end of the Tokugawa period, but they no longer exist. *Maiko* are not prostitutes.

   全く違います。花魁は江戸時代まで存在した公娼で今は存在していません。舞妓は娼妓ではありません。

3. Almost all of them are in Kyoto, and the five most famous areas are Kamishichiken, Ponto-cho, Miyagawa-cho, Gion Kobu, and Gion Higashi.

   ほとんどは京都で、京都の上七軒、先斗町、宮川町、祇園甲部、祇園東の五つの地域が有名です。

11 城

❓ こんな質問をされたら？

1 When were castles first built?

城はいつごろからできましたか？

2 What was the purpose of the castles?

城にはどんな役割がありましたか？

3 What castles are famous?

有名な城にはどんなものがありますか？

弘前城

Castles

 30秒で、こう答えよう！

1 From the ancient to the medieval period, castles were built for military purposes.

古代から中世にかけて、城は軍事目的のために築かれました。

2 In the sixteenth and seventeenth centuries, the role of the castle changed from that of military facility to local government center.

16世紀から17世紀の間に、城の役割は軍事施設から地方行政府へと変貌しました。

3 Himeji Castle is world famous for its beauty. The current castle was completed in 1601. Other notable castles are Matsue in Shimane Prefecture, Hikone in Shiga Prefecture, Inuyama in Aichi Prefecture, Matsumoto in Nagano Prefecture, and Kumamoto in Kumamoto Prefecture.

姫路城は美しさで世界的に有名です。現在の城は1601年に完成しました。他の有名な城としては、島根県の松江城、滋賀県の彦根城、愛知県の犬山城、長野県の松本城、熊本県の熊本城があります。

第2章
Chapter 2

日本の伝統文化の歴史
History of Japanese Traditional Culture

1 日本の演劇

❓ こんな質問をされたら？

1 When did Kabuki first begin?

歌舞伎はいつごろ成立しましたか？

2 When did Noh first begin?

能はいつごろ成立しましたか？

3 When did Bunraku first begin?

文楽はいつごろ成立しましたか？

能面

Japanese Theater

💬 30秒で、こう答えよう！

1 Kabuki is a Japanese performing art developed during the Edo period, and it is the most popular form of traditional theater in Japan.

歌舞伎は江戸時代に発展した日本の舞台演劇で、日本の伝統的な演劇の中でも最も人気があります。

2 Noh is a classic performing art of Japan, and it was created and developed in the thirteenth and fourteenth centuries. Many people say that Noh is quite sophisticated in its minimalism.

能は、日本の古典的な舞台芸能で、13〜14世紀に発展しました。多くの人は能はそのミニマリズムゆえに、洗練されていると言います。

3 Bunraku became famous when Takemoto Gidayu started his own theater in Osaka in the late seventeenth century.

文楽は、17世紀の後半に竹本義太夫が大阪で劇場をはじめたことで、有名になりました。

2 日本の生活文化

❓ こんな質問をされたら？

1 When did the tea ceremony begin?

茶道はいつごろ成立しましたか？

---

2 When did the art of flower arrangement begin?

いけばなはいつごろ成立しましたか？

---

3 What is *Bonsai*?

盆栽とは何ですか？

茶道

Japanese Culture of Everyday Life

 30秒で、こう答えよう!

1 The tea ceremony developed along with Zen and was established in the late sixteenth century by a man named Sen no Rikyu.

茶道は禅とともに発展し、16世紀後半に千利休という人によって確立されました。

2 Ikebana is also called *kado*, and it is traditional Japanese flower arrangement developed in the Muromachi period.

いけばなのことを華道ともいい、この伝統的な日本のフラワーアレンジメントは、室町時代に発展しました。

3 *Bonsai* refers to the cultivation of miniature potted trees. It involves an interesting combination of manipulation of nature while encouraging an appreciation of nature.

盆栽とは、ミニチュア鉢植え栽培のことです。自然そのものへの敬意を促す一方で、自然を操る興味深い融合の世界です。

3 日本の伝統スポーツ

❓ こんな質問をされたら？

1 When did Sumo begin?

相撲はいつごろ成立しましたか？

2 When did Judo begin?

柔道はいつごろ成立しましたか？

3 When did Kendo begin?

剣道とはなんですか？

相撲

Traditional Japanese Sports

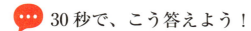 30秒で、こう答えよう！

1 Sumo's origin can be traced back to ancient times. Historically, sumo has close ties with Shinto. Sumo developed as a special type of wrestling performed to worship gods and goddesses.

相撲の起源は、古代まで遡ることができます。歴史的に、相撲は神道と深い関係があります。相撲は神々を崇拝するための特別な取組として発展しました。

2 Judo is a martial art created by Kano Jigoro in 1882. Judo was developed from a classical martial art called *jujutsu*.

柔道は1882年に嘉納治五郎が創始した武道です。柔道は、古くは柔術と呼ばれた武道から派生したものです。

3 Kendo is Japanese sword fighting. Japanese sword fighting techniques became highly developed around the sixteenth century when the country was engulfed in civil war.

剣道は日本の剣術です。日本の剣術の技は、内乱が続いた16世紀頃に発展しました。

4 日本の古典文学

? こんな質問をされたら？

1. What is the *Man'yoshu*?
   万葉集とはなんですか？

2. Could you talk about *The Tale of Genji*?
   源氏物語について教えてください？

3. What did the master of haiku Matsuo Basho write?
   俳句の巨匠松尾芭蕉にはどんな著書がありますか？

松尾芭蕉像

Ancient Japanese Literature

 30秒で、こう答えよう！

1. The *Man'yoshu* is a collection of Japanese verse, poems, and *waka*, which are Japanese poems that follow the pattern of 5-7-5-7-7 syllables. It was edited in the late Nara period. The *Man'yoshu* includes more than 4,500 verses, poems, and *waka* written by people of every rank.

   万葉集とは日本の韻文詩である和歌を集めたもので、和歌とは5-7-5-7-7の音節に則って詠まれた日本の詩のことです。万葉集は奈良時代の終わりに編纂されました。万葉集にはあらゆる地位の人たちによって詠まれた4500首以上の和歌が収められています。

2. *The Tale of Genji*, written by Lady Murasaki Shikibu in the early eleventh century, is considered to be the oldest full-length novel in the world.

   11世紀初期に紫式部によって書かれた『源氏物語』は、世界で最も古い長編小説であると考えられています。

3. His haiku collection called *Oku no Hosomichi*, or *The Narrow Road to the Deep North*, is internationally famous.

   『奥の細道』という俳句集は国際的に有名です。

第2章　日本の伝統文化の歴史

5 日本の古典絵画

❓ こんな質問をされたら？

1 Why were ukiyo-e produced?

なぜ浮世絵がつくられたのですか？

2 What are *Shunga*?

春画とは何ですか？

3 What are mural paintings?

障壁画とはなんですか？

狩野永徳筆　唐獅子図障壁画

Ancient Japanese Pictorial Arts

 30秒で、こう答えよう！

1 Ukiyo-e prints were the equivalent of modern-day picture postcards, posters and pin-ups, as well as book illustrations.

浮世絵版画は、今日の絵葉書、ポスター、ブロマイドや本の挿絵に相当するものだったのです。

2 *Shunga* were erotic prints, meant for both entertainment and instruction.

春画とは、エロチックな版画のことで、娯楽と教育を兼ねたものでした。

3 *Shoheki-ga* are traditional paintings done on sliding paper doors and screens. Such artwork became popular in the Azuchi Momoyama period.

障壁画とは、襖や屏風に描かれる伝統的な絵画のことです。このような芸術作品は安土桃山時代に人気を博しました。

6 日本の宗教

❓ こんな質問をされたら？

1 What is Japan's native religion?
日本固有の宗教はなんですか？

2 When was Buddhism introduced?
仏教はいつごろ日本に入ってきましたか？

3 When did Christianity come to Japan?
キリスト教はいつ日本に入ってきましたか？

Japanese Religions

 30秒で、こう答えよう！

1 The native religion is called Shinto, and places of worship are called *jinja*, or shrines.

それは神道です。礼拝するところは神社と呼ばれます。

2 In 552, an envoy from Baekje brought Buddhism to the Yamato Court. In Yamato, people argued about whether Buddhism should be accepted or not.

552年、百済からの使節が大和朝廷に仏教をもたらしました。大和では、仏教を受け入れるべきか否かで論争になりました。

3 Along with guns, Christianity was brought to Japan in 1549 by Francis Xavier. With the support of Oda Nobunaga, Christianity spread in Japan.

鉄砲とともに、1549年フランシスコ・ザビエルによってキリスト教が日本にもたらされました。織田信長の支持により、キリスト教は日本で広がりました。

第3章
Chapter 3

日本の古代

Ancient Japan

1 先史時代

❓ こんな質問をされたら？

1 When did the Japanese archipelago separate from the Asian continent?

日本列島はいつ頃、アジア大陸から離れたのですか？

2 What was the Jomon period like?

縄文時代とはどんな時代ですか？

3 What was the Yayoi period like?

弥生時代とはどんな時代ですか？

土偶（縄文時代末期）

縄文土器

弥生土器

Prehistoric Period

 30秒で、こう答えよう！

1 Around twelve thousand years ago, the Ice Age came to an end, and Japan was separated from the Asian continent.

約1万2000年前、氷河期が終わり、日本はアジア大陸から離れました。

2 In the Jomon period, people built villages and lived by hunting and fishing.

縄文時代、人々は村を形成し、狩猟や漁によって生活しました。

3 The Yayoi period, between 400 B.C. and the third century A.D., was when Japan began to become united as a nation. It was also the period when rice farming began.

弥生時代とは紀元前400年から3世紀までの期間で、日本が国家として統合され始めた時代です。この時代に米作が始まりました。

2 先史時代の国際交流

❓ こんな質問をされたら？

1 Was there international exchange during the Yayoi period?

弥生時代に国際交流はありましたか？

2 What was *Wa*?

倭とはなんですか？

3 What kind of kingdom was Yamatai?

邪馬台国とはどんな国だったのですか？

漢倭奴国王印

International Relations in the Prehistoric Period

 30秒で、こう答えよう！

1 The Yayoi period was when international exchange with Korea and China started.

弥生時代になって、朝鮮や中国との国際的な交流が始まりました。

---

2 *Wa* was the name used to describe ancient Japan or its people.

倭とは、古代日本やその国民を表す名前です。

---

3 Yamatai-koku was an ancient kingdom that was ruled by Queen Himiko. Queen Himiko sent a mission to China and received a golden seal from the emperor of the Wei Dynasty of China. Archeologists argue about whether Yamatai-koku was in Kyushu or around the area of Nara.

邪馬台国は女王卑弥呼によって統治された古代王国です。女王卑弥呼は中国に使節団を送り、魏王朝の皇帝から金印を授与されました。考古学者たちは、邪馬台国は九州にあったのか、奈良近郊にあったのかで論争しています。

3 大和朝廷の成立

❓ こんな質問をされたら？

1 When was Japan first unified as a country?
日本はいつ頃国家として統一されましたか？

2 What are *kofun* burial mounds?
古墳とはどういうものですか？

3 Which is the largest burial mound?
最も大きい古墳は誰のものですか？

仁徳天皇陵

Establishment of the Yamato Court

 30秒で、こう答えよう!

1 The Kofun period was when Japan was united by the Yamato Court, which was established around the third to fourth century.

古墳時代になって日本は大和朝廷によって統合されましたが、それは約3世紀から4世紀にかけてのことでした。

2 A *kofun* is an ancient tomb for an emperor or a member of a powerful clan. Some *kofun* for emperors of the Yamato Court are huge, and prove how powerful it had become by the fifth century.

古墳とは、天皇や有力な豪族のための古代の墓のことです。大和朝廷の天皇の古墳の中には巨大なものがあり、5世紀までに大和朝廷がいかに権勢を振るったかを証明しています。

3 The *kofun* of Emperor Nintoku is the biggest of all, and it was constructed around the fifth century.

仁徳天皇の古墳は中でも最大で、5世紀頃に造られました。

4 飛鳥時代

❓ こんな質問をされたら？

1 What was the Asuka period like?

飛鳥時代とはどういう時代でしたか？

2 What kind of person was Shotoku Taishi?

聖徳太子とはどういう人物ですか？

3 How were relations with China during this period?

この時代中国とどのような付き合いをしていましたか？

聖徳太子像

Asuka Period

 30 秒で、こう答えよう！

1. The Asuka period was part of the era of the Yamato Court when Buddhist culture prospered. Asuka culture is known for its influence from the Sui and early Tang Dynasties.

   飛鳥時代とは大和時代の一部であり、仏教文化が栄えました。飛鳥文化は隋や唐王朝初期の影響を受けていることで知られています。

2. Prince Shotoku Taishi was the regent of Empress Suiko in the early seventh century. He established the Seventeen-article Constitution, which is Japan's oldest law, and erected Horyu-ji Temple in 607.

   聖徳太子は7世紀初期に推古天皇の摂政をしていました。日本で最古の法律十七条憲法を定め、607年に法隆寺を建立しました。

3. Prince Shotoku dispatched Ono no Imoko as Japan's official envoy to the Sui Dynasty China to request friendly relations.

   聖徳太子は日本の正式な使節として小野妹子を隋に派遣し、友好関係を求めました。

5 大化の改新

? こんな質問をされたら？

1 How did Japanese government change after Shotoku Taishi?

聖徳太子の後、日本の政治はどうなりましたか？

2 What were the Taika Reforms all about?

大化の改新とはどんな出来事ですか？

3 What was Japan's first unified tax system?

日本で最初の統一された税制はなんですか？

神武東征

Taika Reforms

 30秒で、こう答えよう！

1 After the death of Prince Shotoku in 622, there was political turmoil in the Yamato Court. Soga no Iruka and his father became the most powerful figures.

622年の聖徳太子の死後、大和朝廷内で政争が起きました。蘇我入鹿と彼の父親が最高権力者となりました。

2 The Taika Reform was a coup d'état and an attempt to create a centralized nation under the emperor's authority.

大化の改新とはクーデターであり、天皇の権威のもとで中央集権国家を創ろうという試みでした。

3 During the Taika Reform, a new taxation system called *soyocho* was started. *So* was a tax on the rice harvest, *yo* was payment in lieu of labor, and *cho* was payment in kind.

大化の改新の期間に、租庸調という新しい租税制度が始められました。祖は米の収穫に対する税、庸は労役の代わりの支払い、調は現物支給でした。

6 律令制度

❓ こんな質問をされたら？

1 What was the Ritsuryo System of legal codes?
律令制度とは何ですか？

2 What was the Taiho Code?
大宝律令とはどのようなものですか？

3 What is the oldest kind of Japanese coin?
日本最古のお金はなんですか？

和同開珎銀銭

Ritsuryo System

 30秒で、こう答えよう！

1 The Ritsuryo System was based on the centralized government in China. It was used by the Yamato Court to create a strong nation under the rule of the emperor.

律令体制は中国の中央集権政府に基づいたものでした。これは、天皇統治のもとで強い国家を創るために大和朝廷によって採用されました。

2 The *Taiho-ritsuryo*, or Taiho Code, was the first law book in Japan, and it was made in 701. With the Taiho Code, the ancient Japanese administrative and legal system was established.

大宝律令とは日本初の法典であり、701年に制定されました。大宝律令によって、古代日本の行政・司法制度が確立しました。

3 In 708, Japan's first coinage of widespread currency, the *Wado Kaichin*, was minted.

708年に、日本最初の通貨が鋳造されました。広く流通したその通貨は和同開珎といいます。

第4章
Chapter 4

奈良時代
Nara Period

1 平城京

❓ こんな質問をされたら？

1 When did the Nara period begin and end?

奈良時代はいつからいつまでですか？

2 It is said that Buddhism flourished during the Nara period, but what kind of events occurred?

奈良時代には仏教が隆盛したそうですが、具体的にはどのようなことが起こりましたか？

3 Why didn't the Nara period last even 100 years?

奈良時代はなぜ100年もしないうちに終わったのですか？

平城京

Capital City of Heijo-kyo (Nara)

 30秒で、こう答えよう！

1 The Nara period was the era when the nation's capital was located in Nara on and off between 710 and 794. Nara was called Heijo-kyo, and it was the first permanent capital city in Japan's history.

710年から794年の間、首都が奈良に置かれていた時代が奈良時代です。奈良は平城京といわれ、日本史上最初の永続的な都となりました。

2 Emperor Shomu tried to govern the country as a Buddhist state, establishing provincial temples called Kokubun-ji. Emperor Shomu also built Todai-ji Temple, which houses the Great Buddha of Nara.

聖武天皇は仏教国家として国を治めようとしました。そこで、国分寺と呼ばれる寺を地方に建てました。聖武天皇はまた、東大寺を建立しました。ここには、奈良の大仏が祀られています。

3 In the late eighth century, Buddhist monks became so powerful that they were able to put a lot of political pressure on the imperial court.

8世紀の終わりになると、僧侶は強大な権力を持つようになり、朝廷に政治的な圧力を掛けることができるようになりました。

2 遣唐使

❓ こんな質問をされたら？

1 What were the missions to China during the Tang dynasty?

遣唐使とは何ですか？

2 What did these missions bring about in Japan?

遣唐使は日本に何をもたらしましたか？

3 What treasures did the envoys bring back from China?

遣唐使が持ち帰った宝物はどこにありますか？

正倉院正倉

Missions to China in the Tang Dynasty

 30秒で、こう答えよう！

1 *Kentoshi* were the missions sent to the Tang Dynasty to learn about their civilization.

遣唐使とは文明を学ぶために唐王朝に派遣された使節団でした。

2 The knowledge and technologies gained by the *kentoshi* were not just from China but from Islamic and Western countries as well.

遣唐使によって得られた知識と技術は、中国からのものだけではなく、イスラムや西洋諸国からももたらされました。

3 The treasure house called Shoso-in was built in the Nara period and contains items from as far away as Persia.

正倉院という宝物殿は奈良時代に建立されましたが、遥かペルシアからの品々も収納されています。

第4章 奈良時代

3 日本正史の誕生

❓ こんな質問をされたら？

1 What kind of work is the *Kojiki*?

『古事記』とはどういう書物ですか？

2 What kind of work is the *Nihon Shoki*?

『日本書紀』とはどういう書物ですか？

3 What is the *Fudoki*?

『風土記』とはなんですか？

『古事記』
（真福寺収蔵・国宝）

Birth of Japanese Official Histories

 30秒で、こう答えよう！

1 The *Kojiki*, or *Record of Ancient Matters*, is a book compiled in 712 to record the legends and oral history of ancient Japan. The *Kojiki* records the succession of emperors and various myths as passed down through oral tradition from ancient times.

『古事記』は712年に編纂された本で、古代日本の伝説や口述の歴史を記録しています。『古事記』には、古代から口述で伝えられてきた、天皇の継承やさまざまな神話が記録されています。

2 The *Nihon Shoki* was compiled in 720 as a formal historical record to tell how the imperial court had been established.

『日本書紀』は720年に正式な歴史の記録として編纂され、朝廷がどのようにして確立したかを述べています。

3 The *Fudoki*, or *Records of the culture and geography of provinces of Japan*, was compiled in 713 to tell the legends, folklore, and history of the provinces of ancient Japan.

『風土記』は713年に編纂され、古代日本の地方の伝説、民話、歴史について書かれています。

第5章
Chapter 5

平安時代

Heian Period

1 平安京

❓ こんな質問をされたら？

1 Where was the Heian capital? When did the Heian period begin and end?

平安京はどこにありましたか？ また平安時代はいつ始まりいつ終わりましたか？

2 What happened in Buddhism during the Heian period?

平安時代の仏教はどうなりましたか？

3 Did missions to China fluctuate?

遣唐使はどうなりましたか？

東大寺大仏殿

Heian Capital (Kyoto)

💬 30秒で、こう答えよう！

1 Heian-kyo was the ancient capital located in Kyoto. The Heian period was the era between 794 and 1192 when the imperial court was active in Kyoto.

平安京とは京都に置かれた古代の都でした。平安時代とは794年から1192年まで朝廷が京都で機能していた時代を指します。

2 Konin-Jogan culture influenced by Mahayana Buddhism brought from Tang Dynasty China flourished around the ninth century. In the ninth century, there were many temples erected on remote mountains.

中国の唐王朝からもたらされた大乗仏教の影響を受けた弘仁貞観文化が9世紀頃に栄えました。9世紀になると、多くの寺が人里離れた山々に建立されました。

3 *Kentoshi*, or periodic missions to China, were stopped in 894 due to the decline of the Tang Dynasty.

中国への定期的な使節団であった遣唐使は、唐王朝が衰退したため、894年に廃止されました。

2 藤原氏

❓ こんな質問をされたら？

1 What is the origin of the Fujiwara clan?

藤原氏の出自はどこですか？

2 What did the Fujiwara clan do during the Heian period?

平安時代の藤原氏はどうなりましたか？

3 What are *sessho* (regents) and *kanpaku* (chancellors)?

摂政、関白とはどのような人ですか？

藤原氏の代表的な家紋「下がり藤」

The Fujiwara Clan

 30秒で、こう答えよう！

1 The Fujiwara clan was one of the major clans serving the court in the ancient era, and their ancestors had played an important role in achieving the Taika Reform.

藤原氏は古代に朝廷に仕えた有力氏族の一つでした。その先祖は大化の改新を遂行するにあたって重要な役割を演じました。

2 In the tenth century, the Fujiwara clan became powerful enough to become the regents and chief advisors to the emperors.

10世紀になると藤原氏は強大な権力を持つようになり、天皇の後見人、あるいは主席顧問にまでなりました。

3 *Sessho* is the English equivalent of "regent," and *kanpaku* is the role of "chief advisor to the emperor." These powerful roles were dominated by the Fujiwara clan in the Heian period.

摂政とは「天皇の後見人」のことで、関白とは「天皇に対する主席顧問」のような役割です。このような権力のある役割は平安時代に藤原氏によって支配されてきました。

3 平安文学

❓ こんな質問をされたら？

1 In addition to *The Tale of Genji*, what other important works of literature are there in this period?

『源氏物語』のほかに代表的な平安文学はありますか？

2 What are the characteristic features of Heian literature?

平安文学の特徴は何ですか？

3 Would you please explain the Kokin Wakashu?

『古今和歌集』とは何ですか？

清少納言（枕草子絵詞）

Heian Literature

 30秒で、こう答えよう！

1. Another example from the Heian period which is still widely known today is a book called *Makura no Soshi*, or the *Pillow Book*. Like *The Tale of Genji*, it was also written by a woman writer, named Sei Shonagon.

   現在でもよく知られる平安時代の作品として、『枕草子』があります。『源氏物語』と同じく、書いたのは清少納言という女性です。

2. The direct expression of inner feelings and affections in poetry shown in the novels and essays still attracts and appeals to us.

   小説や随筆に出てくる歌に詠まれた直接的な感情や愛情表現は、いまでも魅力的で訴えるものがあります。

3. In the Heian period, the nobles exchanged *waka*, or Japanese poems, to communicate with their lovers. The *Kokin Wakashu* was compiled by Kino Tsurayuki in 905 and is a collection of *waka* produced in the early Heian period.

   平安時代、貴族たちは愛人とコミュニケーションするときに和歌を交わしました。『古今和歌集』は 905 年に紀貫之によって編纂されたもので、平安初期に詠まれた和歌集です。

4 平安仏教

❓ こんな質問をされたら？

1 What is the idea of *Mappo*?

末法思想とは何ですか？

---

2 Why was this pessimistic idea common in the Heian period?

なぜ平安時代に厭世感が漂うこの思想が流行ったのですか？

---

3 Why did Buddhism become popular due to the ideas of *Mappo*?

末法思想で仏教が流行ったのはなぜですか？

東大寺盧遮那仏像

Heian Buddhism

 30秒で、こう答えよう!

1 *Mappo*, or the Third Age of Buddhism, began in 1052. It was believed that during this period, the power of Buddha was in decline and that people would suffer if they were not saved.

末法、すなわち仏教でいう第三段階にあたる時代が1052年に始まりました。この時期、釈迦の力が衰退し、救済されていない人々は被害を被るであろうと信じられていました。

2 Social problems caused by battles, famine, and poverty convinced people that the *Mappo* period had come.

戦いや飢饉や貧困によって引き起こされた社会問題によって、人々は末法期に入ったと確信したのです。

3 The belief in the *Mappo* period stimulated people to long for happiness after death. This was one of the causes of the popularity of the belief in Amida Buddha.

末法思想によって刺激された人々は、死後の幸せを望むようになりました。これが、仏教信仰が広まった理由の一つです。

5 武士の台頭

❓ こんな質問をされたら？

1 Who exactly were the samurai?

武士とはどのような人たちですか？

---

2 What was the relationship between the samurai and the nobility?

武士と貴族の関係は？

---

3 What was the relationship between the samurai and the Imperial Court?

武士と朝廷の関係は？

平家の紋　揚羽蝶

Rise of the Samurai (Warrior Class)

 30秒で、こう答えよう！

1 Samurai warriors were called *bushi* in Japanese, and it was they who gradually organized into fighting forces during the Heian period.

戦士のことを日本語で武士といいます。平安時代に軍隊のようなものを徐々に組織していったのは武士でした。

2 While the Fujiwara clan prospered at the imperial court, many other aristocrats moved to the country and mixed with the local warriors.

藤原氏が朝廷で栄華を誇る一方、他の多くの貴族たちは田舎へ移住し、地方の武士たちと交わっていきました。

3 In the Heian period, warriors in the rural areas were often hired by the central government to protect the imperial court and its interests in the outlying areas.

平安時代、地方の武士たちは頻繁に朝廷に雇われ、朝廷や地方の豪族を護衛していました。

6 平安時代の武装勢力

❓ こんな質問をされたら？

1 What was the lineage of the Genji clan?

源氏とはどういう家系ですか？

2 What was the lineage of the Heike clan?

平家とはどういう家系ですか？

3 Who were the warrior monks?

僧兵とはなんだったのですか？

僧兵弁慶と源義経

Armed Power in the Heian Period

 30秒で、こう答えよう！

1. The Genji is the name of a group of warriors led by the Minamoto clan, and they expanded their influence in the Kanto area. The Minamoto clan were the descendants of Emperor Seiwa from the ninth century.

   源氏とは源一族によって率いられた武家集団の名前で、関東地方に影響力を広げていました。源氏は９世紀の清和天皇の子孫でした。

2. The Heike is the name of a group of warriors led by the Taira clan, and they expanded their influence in western Japan. The Taira clan were the descendants of Emperor Kanmu, who founded Heian-kyo in 795.

   平家とは平一族によって率いられた武家集団の名前で、西日本で影響力を広げていました。平家は795年に平安京を築いた桓武天皇の子孫でした。

3. *Sohei* were warriors who fought for major temples. The *sohei* warriors of Enryaku-ji Temple in Kyoto became very powerful.

   僧兵は大きな寺のために闘った戦士でした。京都の延暦寺の僧兵は強大な勢力を持ちました。

7 院政と保元・平治の乱

❓ こんな質問をされたら？

1 What is government by a retired emperor, called *insei*?

院政とはどういう政治ですか？

---

2 What kind of conflict was the Hogen Disturbance?

保元の乱はどのような戦いですか？

---

3 What resulted from the Heiji Disturbance?

平治の乱とは？その結果は？

源氏の紋　笹竜胆

Insei and the Hogen/Heiji Disturbance

 30秒で、こう答えよう！

1. The *insei* system was begun by the retired Emperor Shirakawa in 1086 and caused another conflict between the emperor and the *jo-ko*, or retired emperor, in the twelfth century.

   院政は1086年に退位した白河天皇によって始められましたが、12世紀になると天皇と退位した天皇である上皇との間に新たな衝突を引き起こすことになりました。

2. In 1156, due to a conflict over the succession of the emperor, the Hogen Disturbance broke out. The Genji and the Heike played influential roles as military forces.

   1156年、皇位継承を巡る衝突で保元の乱が起こりました。源氏と平家は武家集団として重要な役割を果たしました。

3. The Heiji Disturbance was fought in 1159. The lord of the Heike, a man named Taira no Kiyomori, defeated the Genji.

   1159年平治の乱が起こりました。平家の主君である平清盛が源氏を打ち破りました。

8 平家の繁栄と滅亡

❓ こんな質問をされたら？

1 What was the period of the Heike like?

平家の時代はどんな時代でしたか？

2 Why were the Heike overthrown?

平家はなぜ滅んだのですか？

3 Why is Minamoto Yoshitsune, the hero who conquered the Taira, called a tragic hero?

平家討伐のヒーロー源義経はなぜ悲劇のヒーローと呼ばれるのですか？

赤間神宮にある平家一門の墓

壇ノ浦古戦場址

Flourishing and Decline of the Heike

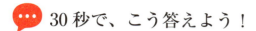 30秒で、こう答えよう!

1 The Heike enjoyed their prosperity and acted like noble aristocrats, supported by their military power.

平家はその軍事力によって栄華を享受し、高貴な貴族のように振る舞いました。

2 The Genji survivors gradually re-formed and the Heike were defeated by Minamoto no Yoshitsune of the Genji clan in 1186 at the battle of Dan no Ura, off the coast of what is now Shimonoseki.

源氏の生き残りは徐々に再生し、1186年、平家は現在の下関の沿岸にある壇ノ浦の戦いで源義経に敗れました。

3 Minamoto no Yoshitsune's older brother Minamoto no Yoritomo, the leader of the Genji, became cautious of him. Minamoto no Yoshitsune escaped to the domain of the Fujiwara in Tohoku, where he was killed by one of the Fujiwaras.

源氏のリーダーであり、義経の兄である源頼朝は義経に不信感をいだきました。源義経は東北の藤原氏の領土に逃げますが、そこで藤原氏の一人に殺されてしまいました。

第6章
Chapter 6

鎌倉時代
Kamakura Period

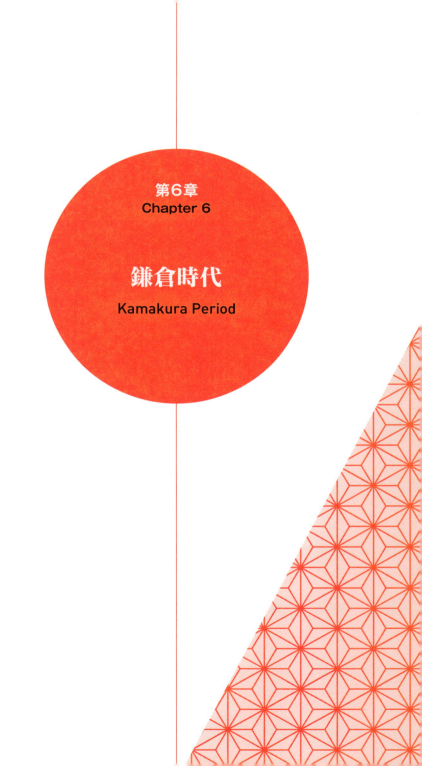

1 源氏と北条氏

❓ こんな質問をされたら？

1 When was the Kamakura Shogunate established?

鎌倉幕府はいつ成立しましたか？

2 How did the Hojo clan gain political power?

北条氏はどうやって政権を獲得したのですか？

3 What is the meaning of *gokenin*, *shugo* and *jito*?

「御家人」「守護」「地頭」とは何だったのですか？

源 頼朝

The Minamoto and the Hojo

 30秒で、こう答えよう！

1. After defeating the Heike, Minamoto no Yoritomo was appointed shogun, or supreme general, and he established a government in Kamakura in 1192.

   平家を滅ぼすと、源頼朝は将軍、すなわち征夷大将軍に任命され、1192年鎌倉に幕府を興しました。

2. After the third shogun was assassinated, the Hojo clan took control of the government as regents.

   3代将軍が暗殺されると、北条氏は執権として幕府を牛耳りました。

3. *Gokenin* were retainers serving as warriors for the Kamakura Shogunate. *Shugo* were officials who were appointed to govern outlying provinces by the shogunate. *Jito* were local land stewards appointed by the shogunate.

   御家人とは鎌倉幕府のために戦士として仕えた家来でした。守護とは、諸国を統治するために幕府によって任命された行政官でした。地頭とは幕府によって任命された地方の荘園の管理官でした。

2 承久の乱

❓ こんな質問をされたら？

1 What was the cause of the Jokyu Disturbance?

承久の乱の原因はなんですか？

---

2 How did the Jokyu Disturbance evolve?

承久の乱はどのように展開しましたか？

---

3 What resulted from the Jokyu Disturbance?

承久の乱の結果どうなりましたか？

承久の乱後、壱岐島に流罪となった後鳥羽上皇

Jokyu Disturbance

 30秒で、こう答えよう！

1 Since there were two powers, the shogunate government and the imperial court, the imperial court tried to recover their position by destroying the Kamakura Shogunate.

幕府と朝廷という2つの勢力が存在していたので、朝廷は鎌倉幕府を滅ぼして地位の奪還を図りました。

2 In 1221, the imperial court and the Kamakura Shogunate fought in Kyoto, and the imperial court was defeated by the shogunate, led by the Hojo clan.

1221年、朝廷と鎌倉幕府は京都で戦い、北条氏が率いる幕府に朝廷は敗れてしまいます。

3 As a result of the Jokyu Disturbance, the Kamakura Shogunate became the real administrative power under the authority of the imperial court.

承久の乱の結果、鎌倉幕府は朝廷の認可のもと実際の行政力を持つようになりました。

3 元寇

❓ こんな質問をされたら？

1 What caused the Mongol Invasions?

元寇の原因はなんですか？

2 How did the Mongol Invasion evolve?

元寇はどのように展開しましたか？

3 What resulted from the Mongol Invasions?

元寇の結果どうなりましたか？

蒙古襲来絵詞

Mongol Invasions

 30秒で、こう答えよう！

1. The Mongolian Emperor Kublai Khan began the Yuan Dynasty in China in 1271 and asked Japan to join his empire. When the Kamakura Shogunate refused the request of the Mongolian Empire, they sent troops to Kyushu in 1274 and 1281.

   モンゴル帝国の皇帝フビライ・ハーンは1271年に中国で元王朝を始め、日本に自分の帝国に入るように求めました。鎌倉幕府がモンゴル帝国の要求を拒むと1274年と1281年に九州に軍隊を派遣しました。

2. Both massive invasions failed because their ships were destroyed by typhoons along with strong military resistance.

   2つの大規模な侵攻は強い軍事的抵抗のうえに、船団が台風で破壊されたことにより、失敗に終わりました。

3. Defending against the Mongolian invasion cost the Kamakura shogunate a fortune, and the *gokenin* who fought for the shogun faced a financial crisis.

   モンゴルの侵攻を防ぐために鎌倉幕府には膨大な費用がかかりました。そして、幕府のために戦った御家人たちは財務危機に直面しました。

第6章 鎌倉時代

4 鎌倉文学

❓ こんな質問をされたら？

1 What are the characteristics of Kamakura literature?

鎌倉文学の特徴はなんですか？

2 Why was Fujiwara no Teika an important literary figure?

なぜ藤原定家は文学の上で重要人物とされたのですか？

3 What are the famous *zuihitsu* that were first created in this period?

この時期に書かれた著名な随筆を教えてください。

吉田兼好

Kamakura Literature

 30秒で、こう答えよう！

1 Many works of literature and arts were influenced by *Mappo* and Buddhist longing for happiness after death.

末法や死後の幸福を希求する仏教に影響された多くの文芸、芸術作品が生まれました。

2 Fujiwara no Teika was famous as the poet who compiled the *waka* collection called the *Shin Kokin Wakashu*.

藤原定家は『新古今和歌集』という和歌集を編纂した歌人として有名でした。

3 Kamo no Chomei was a monk and poet of the early Kamakura period. His essay titled *Hojoki*, or *The Ten Foot Square Hut*, is well known among Japanese people. Yoshida Kenko was a monk and poet of the Kamakura period. His essays entitled *Tsurezure-Gusa* or *Essays in Idleness* are considered a gem of medieval Japanese literature.

鴨長明は鎌倉初期の僧侶であり歌人でしたが、『方丈記』という随筆は日本人には有名です。吉田兼好は鎌倉時代の僧であり歌人でした。『徒然草』という彼の随筆は中世日本文学の宝石と考えられています。

5 鎌倉仏教

❓ こんな質問をされたら？

1 Why did the Jodo-shinshu Buddhist sect become so well established during the Kamakura period?

浄土真宗はなぜ鎌倉時代に広く信じられるようになったのですか？

2 What is Zen Buddhism like?

禅宗とはどのような仏教ですか？

3 What is Nichiren Buddhism like?

日蓮宗とはどのような仏教ですか？

日蓮上人像

Kamakura Buddhism

 30秒で、こう答えよう！

1 Since the theory of Jodo-shinshu was so simple and guaranteed that anybody who believed in Amida Buddha could be saved, it was accepted by many people.

浄土真宗の教えは非常に簡単であり、阿弥陀仏を信じるものは誰でも救われることを保証していたので、多くの人々に受け入れられました。

2 Zen was a popular belief system among the samurai class in feudal times because it required people to develop internal strength through stoic training.

禅宗は封建時代に武士階級の間で人気の信仰でした。というのも、禁欲的な修行によって精神力を高めることを求めたからです。

3 Nichiren-shu is a Buddhist sect started by a priest named Nichiren in the thirteenth century. Nichiren believed that if people recited the Lotus Sutra, they would become enlightened.

日蓮宗は、13世紀に日蓮という僧によって興された宗派です。日蓮は法華経を唱えさえすれば悟りを開けると信じていました。

6 鎌倉幕府の崩壊と建武の新政

❓ こんな質問をされたら？

1 When did the Kamakura Shogunate collapse?

鎌倉幕府はいつ滅びましたか？

2 What was the new Kenmu government like?

建武の新政とはどのような政治ですか？

3 Why was the new government brought to a standstill?

建武の新政はどうして頓挫したのですか？

後醍醐天皇

Collapse of the Kamakura Shogunate and the Kenmu Restoration

 30秒で、こう答えよう！

1 In 1333, Emperor Go-Daigo and Nitta Yoshisada, a powerful *gokenin*, attacked Kamakura and destroyed both the Hojo clan and the Kamakura Shogunate.

1333年、後醍醐天皇と有力な御家人である新田義貞は鎌倉を攻撃し、北条氏と幕府を倒しました。

2 *Kenmu no Shinsei*, or the Kenmu Restoration, was initiated by Emperor Go-Daigo in 1333 after the overthrow of the Kamakura Shogunate. Emperor Go-Daigo tried to restore the government of the emperor and nobles.

建武の新政は鎌倉幕府崩壊後、1333年に後醍醐天皇によって始められました。後醍醐天皇は天皇と貴族の政府を再建しようとしました。

3 The Kenmu Restoration failed in two years when samurai led by Ashikaga Takauji defeated the troops of Emperor Go-Daigo.

足利尊氏が率いた侍が後醍醐天皇の軍隊を打ち負かし、建武の新政は2年で頓挫しました。

第7章
Chapter 7

室町時代
Muromachi Period

1 室町幕府と南北朝

こんな質問をされたら？

1 What kind of person was Ashikaga Takauji?

足利尊氏とはどのような人物ですか

2 What was the period of Northern and Southern Courts like?

南北朝とはどのような時代ですか？

3 How was the matter of the Northern and Southern Courts cleared up?

南北朝はいつ解消されましたか？

足利尊氏

Muromachi Shogunate and the Northern and Southern Courts

 30秒で、こう答えよう！

1 Ashikaga Takauji was the son of a powerful *gokenin* who served the Hojo clan during the Kamakura Shogunate, who established the Muromachi Shogunate in Kyoto in 1336.

足利尊氏は鎌倉幕府で北条氏に仕えた有力御家人の子でした。1336年京都に室町幕府を興しました。

2 The period when the Muromachi Shogunate and the court located at Yoshino confronted each other is called the *Nanboku-cho jidai*, or the Northern and Southern Courts period. Japan was divided in two.

室町幕府と吉野の朝廷が互いに衝突した時代は南北朝時代と呼ばれます。日本は2つに分断されました。

3 When Ashikaga Yoshimitsu was in power, the Southern Court gave up, and the Nanboku-cho period came to an end in 1392.

足利義満が権力の座にあったとき南朝は継続をあきらめ、1392年南北朝時代は終焉を迎えました。

2 北山文化

? こんな質問をされたら？

1 When did Kitayama culture flourish?

北山文化はいつ繁栄しましたか？

2 What was the ideological background of Kitayama culture?

北山文化の思想的背景は？

3 How were Noh and Kyogen established?

能、狂言はどのようにして成立しましたか？

金閣寺

Kitayama Culture

💬 30秒で、こう答えよう！

1 Kitayama culture was the Buddhist culture which bloomed in the era of Ashikaga Yoshimitsu. Kinkaku-ji Temple in Kyoto is a typical example of Kitayama culture.

北山文化は仏教文化で足利義満の時代に開花しました。京都金閣寺は北山文化の典型例です。

2 In particular, thoughts and concepts from Zen were widely adopted in architecture and gardens around the era of Ashikaga Yoshimitsu.

特に、禅の思想や哲学は足利義満の時代に建築や庭園に広く取り入れられました。

3 Noh and Kyogen were established as performing arts with the support of Ashikaga Yoshimitsu.

能や狂言は足利義満の保護を受けて芸能として成立しました。

3 倭寇と応仁の乱

❓ こんな質問をされたら？

1 Who were the pirates known as *wako*?

倭寇とはなんですか？

2 What kind of conflict was the Onin War?

応仁の乱とはどうのような戦争ですか？

3 What resulted from the Onin War?

応仁の乱の結果どうなりましたか？

「応仁の乱勃発地」の石碑

Wako Pirates and the Onin War

 30秒で、こう答えよう！

1 *Wako* were Japanese pirates who raided the coastlines of Korea and China and were quite active between the thirteenth and fifteenth centuries.

倭冦とは朝鮮や中国沿岸に侵犯した日本人の海賊で、13世紀から15世紀にかけて、非常に活動的でした。

2 The Onin War was a series of battles between the Hosokawa and the Yamana clans which lasted for eleven years in Kyoto.

応仁の乱とは細川氏と山名氏の間の一連の戦いで、京都で11年間続きました。

3 Many parts of Kyoto were destroyed, and the power of the shogun was severely weakened during the Onin War. After the Onin War, Japan fell into a period of civil war.

応仁の乱の間に京都のほとんどが破壊され、将軍の勢力は極端に弱まりました。応仁の乱後、日本は内戦の時代に陥りました。

4 東山文化

こんな質問をされたら？

1 What was Higashiyama culture like?

東山文化とはどのような文化ですか？

2 What are the characteristics of Higashiyama culture?

東山文化の特徴はどのようなものですか？

3 Where can we discover Higashiyama culture?

東山文化はどこに見られますか？

銀閣寺

Higashiyama Culture

💬 30秒で、こう答えよう！

1 Higashiyama culture was the wartime culture created by the artists who escaped from Kyoto. Ginkaku-ji Temple is a typical example of Higashiyama culture.

東山文化とは京都を逃れた芸術家によって創られた戦時中の文化です。銀閣寺は東山文化の典型例です。

2 The concepts of *wabi*, *sabi*, and *yugen* expressed in gardens, fine arts, and performing arts were established in the Higashiyama cultural movement.

庭園、芸術、芸能で表現された侘び、寂び、幽玄という概念は東山文化の動きの中で確立されました。

3 *Sado*, or the tea ceremony, Zen gardens, and many other refined and beautiful things that you can still enjoy were developed during the flowering of Higashiyama culture.

茶道や禅庭、他にも多くの洗練された美しい物事は今なお楽しむことができますが、それらは東山文化が開花したときに発展しました。

第7章 室町時代

5 戦国時代

❓ こんな質問をされたら？

1 What was the Period of Warring States like?

戦国時代とはどのような時代ですか？

2 What was *gekokujo*, where the low dominate the high?

下剋上とはなんですか？

3 How did the *sengoku daimyo* (warlords) evolve?

戦国大名はどのようにして成立したのですか？

戦国大名　上杉謙信

Period of Warring States

 30秒で、こう答えよう！

1. The *Sengoku jidai* was the time during the Muromachi period when Japan was thrown into a chaotic civil war.

   戦国時代とは室町時代の中で日本が混沌とした内戦状態に入った時代のことです。

2. *Gekokujo* is a phrase which describes a rebellion to take over a domain or the interests of one's superiors. In the Warring States period, many lords were overthrown after rebellions by their subordinates.

   下克上とは、目上の者の領地や利益を奪い取るための反乱を表わす言葉です。戦国時代に、多くの守護大名は家臣の反乱で引きずりおろされました。

3. After a series of *gekokujo*, many lords were overthrown. In the sixteenth century, Japan was divided up by major daimyo, or feudal lords, who survived the civil war.

   一連の下克上により、多くの大名は権力の座から降ろされました。16世紀に日本は内戦を生き延びた戦国大名によって分割されました。

6 戦国大名 その1

❓ こんな質問をされたら？

1 What kind of person was Takeda Shingen?

武田信玄とはどのような人物ですか？

2 What kind of person was Uesugi Kenshin?

上杉謙信とはどのような人物ですか？

3 What was The Battle of Kawanaka-jima?

川中島の合戦とは？

川中島の合戦

Warlords of the Warring States Period

 30秒で、こう答えよう！

1. Takeda Shingen was one of the well-known daimyo in the Warring States period, and had a powerful territory in the current Yamanashi and Nagano prefectures during the mid sixteenth century.

   武田信玄は戦国時代の有名な大名の一人で16世紀半ば現在の山梨や長野に強大な領地を持っていました。

2. Uesugi Kenshin was a rival of Takeda Shingen who took over Echigo, which is now Niigata Prefecture.

   上杉謙信は武田信玄のライバルで、今の新潟県である越後を領地としていました。

3. The Battle of Kawanaka-jima was a series of famous battles between Takeda Shingen and Uesugi Kenshin near what is now Nagano City.

   川中島の合戦とは武田信玄と上杉謙信による一連の有名な戦いで、今の長野市近郊で行われました。

7 戦国大名 その2

? こんな質問をされたら？

1 What kind of person was Hojo Soun?
北条早雲とはどのような人物ですか？

2 What kind of person was Mori Motonari?
毛利元就とはどのような人物ですか？

3 What kind of person was Date Masamune?
伊達政宗とはどのような人物ですか？

小田原城

Warlords of the Warring States Period

💬 30秒で、こう答えよう！

1. Hojo Soun was a powerful daimyo in the mid sixteenth century who united the southern Kanto area. His headquarters was at Odawara Castle.

   北条早雲は16世紀半ばの有力大名で南関東を統合しました。その本丸は小田原城にありました。

2. Mori Motonari was a famous daimyo who united the Chugoku area in the mid sixteenth century.

   毛利元就は16世紀半ばに中国地方を統治した有名な大名でした。

3. Date Masamune was a powerful daimyo who expanded his territory in what is now Miyagi Prefecture in the Tohoku area.

   伊達政宗は東北地方の現在の宮城県で領土を拡大した有力大名でした。

第7章 室町時代

8 西洋との出会い

❓ こんな質問をされたら？

1 How did Christianity develop in Japan?

キリスト教は日本でどのように発展しましたか？

2 When were firearms introduced to Japan?

鉄砲はいつ日本にもたらされましたか？

3 What were the merchants of Sakai like?

堺商人とはどのような人たちですか？

フランシスコ・ザビエル

Encounters with the West

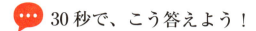 30秒で、こう答えよう！

1 Along with guns, Christianity was brought to Japan in 1549 by Francis Xavier. In 1582, some daimyo who had converted to Christianity sent an envoy to Rome.

鉄砲とともに、1549年フランシスコ・ザビエルによってキリスト教が日本にもたらされました。1582年、キリスト教に改宗した大名はローマに使節を派遣しました。

2 In 1543, when a Portuguese ship landed at Tanegashima, one of the southern islands of Kagoshima Prefecture, guns were introduced to Japan. The introduction of guns changed the way that samurai fought.

1543年、ポルトガル船が鹿児島県の南の島の一つである種子島に到着したとき、鉄砲が日本に紹介されました。鉄砲の伝来は侍の戦い方を変えました。

3 The merchants of Sakai, in the southern area of Osaka, sold guns and other Western goods and became powerful, similar to their counterparts in Venice, in Italy.

大阪の南部にある堺の商人は、鉄砲や西洋の他の商品を売って力をつけました。まさに、イタリアのベニスの商人と同様です。

第8章
Chapter 8

安土桃山時代

Azuchi Momoyama Period

1 戦国時代の終了

❓ こんな質問をされたら？

1 When did the Muromachi Shogunate collapse?

室町幕府はいつ滅びましたか？

---

2 What was the Azuchi Momoyama Period like?

安土桃山時代はどんな時代ですか？

---

3 How did relations with the West change?

西洋との関係はどうなりましたか？

織田信長（狩野元秀画）

End of the Period of Warring States

💬 30秒で、こう答えよう！

1 Oda Nobunaga finally exiled the last shogun of the Ashikaga clan from Kyoto in 1573 and overthrew the Muromachi Shogunate.

織田信長は1573年についに足利氏の最後の将軍を京都から追放し、室町幕府を転覆させました。

2 The Azuchi Momoyama era was between 1573 and 1603, and it was the time in which Oda Nobunaga and Toyotomi Hideyoshi became powerful leaders in Japan.

安土桃山時代は1573年から1603年の間で、織田信長と豊臣秀吉が日本の強大なリーダーとなった時代でした。

3 The Azuchi Momoyama period was a time when the trade relationship between Japan and Western nations flourished.

安土桃山時代になって、日本と西洋諸国との貿易は繁栄しました。

第8章 安土桃山時代

2 織田信長

❓ こんな質問をされたら？

1 What kind of person was Oda Nobunaga?

織田信長はどんな人物でしたか？

2 What did Oda Nobunaga do?

織田信長はどのようなことをしましたか？

3 Why did Nobunaga's administration collapse?

織田政権はどうして滅んだのですか？

延暦寺

Oda Nobunaga

💬 30秒で、こう答えよう！

1 Oda Nobunaga is one of the most popular heroes in Japanese history because of his strong character and his challenging of the traditions of the old world.

織田信長は、その強烈な個性と古い伝統に立ち向かう姿により、日本の歴史上、最も人気のあるヒーローの一人となっています。

2 Oda Nobunaga expanded his territory and suppressed Ikko-shu, attacking and burning Enryaku-ji Temple, which was a big political threat.

織田信長は領地を拡大し、延暦寺を攻撃し燃やすことによって一向宗を鎮圧しました。彼らは政治的に大きな脅威となっていたからです。

3 In June of 1582, Oda Nobunaga was betrayed and killed by Akechi Mitsuhide, one of his most powerful generals, at Honno-ji Temple in Kyoto.

1582年6月、織田信長は京都の本能寺で、最も有力な家臣の一人であった明智光秀に裏切られ、殺されました。

第8章 安土桃山時代

3 豊臣秀吉

❓ こんな質問をされたら？

1 What kind of person was Toyotomi Hideyoshi?

豊臣秀吉はどんな人物でしたか？

---

2 How did Toyotomi Hideyoshi unify the country?

豊臣秀吉はどうやって天下を統一しましたか？

---

3 What was Hideyoshi's private life like?

秀吉の私生活はどんな風でしたか？

豊臣秀吉（狩野光信画）

Toyotomi Hideyoshi

💬 30秒で、こう答えよう！

1 Toyotomi Hideyoshi was hired by Oda Nobunaga in 1554 and was promoted extraordinarily quickly because of his great talent.

豊臣秀吉は1554年に織田信長に登用され、天賦の才によって異例の早さで出世しました。

2 Hideyoshi became the successor of Oda Nobunaga by defeating his rivals after killing Akechi Mitsuhide. Toyotomi Hideyoshi finally defeated the Hojo clan at Odawara to unite Japan in 1590.

秀吉は明智光秀の殺害後、ライバルたちを打ち負かし、織田信長の後継者となりました。1590年に小田原の北条氏を打ち負かし、ついに日本を統一しました。

3 Toyotomi Hideyoshi loved his mistress, Yodogimi, the niece of Oda Nobunaga, and their son became the successor of Toyotomi Hideyoshi.

豊臣秀吉は織田信長の姪である側室の淀君を寵愛していました。そして二人の息子が豊臣秀吉の継承者となりました。

第8章 安土桃山時代

4 秀吉の政策

❓ こんな質問をされたら？

1 When was Osaka Castle built?

大坂城はいつできたのですか？

---

2 It is said that taxation was stabilized during this period, but how did the government do that?

この時代に租税が安定したとされますが、どういう政策をしたのですか？

---

3 What was the policy of the "sword hunt"?

刀狩とはどういう政策ですか？

大阪城

Hideyoshi's Government

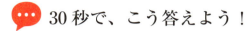

1 Hideyoshi erected Osaka Castle as his headquarters in 1583.

秀吉は1583年、拠城として大坂城を造りました。

2 The *Taiko Kenchi* land survey established the amount of taxes to be paid in each area and created a distinction between the warriors and farmers.

太閤検地によって各地区での租税の支払額が制定され、兵農分離がなされました。

3 *Katanagari* was the policy of seizing the swords possessed by farmers. Toyotomi Hideyoshi tried to separate the samurai into a higher class than the farmers.

刀狩とは農民が所有する刀を奪い取る政策でした。豊臣秀吉は侍を農民よりも高い地位へ分離しようとしました。

5 朝鮮出兵

❓ こんな質問をされたら？

1 What were the invasions of Korea?

朝鮮出兵とは何ですか？

---

2 Why is it said that Imari and other porcelain works developed because of this conflict?

この戦争で、伊万里などで陶磁器が発達したといいますが、どういうことですか？

---

3 How did these conflicts conclude and what were the results?

この戦争はどう収束し、どんな結果をもたらしましたか？

伊万里焼

Invasions of Korea

💬 **30秒で、こう答えよう!**

1 Toyotomi Hideyoshi declared war against the Ming Dynasty of China and invaded Korea.

豊臣秀吉は中国の明朝に宣戦布告し、朝鮮を侵略しました。

2 When Toyotomi Hideyoshi's troops invaded Korea, they brought back many porcelain makers to promote industry in Kyushu.

豊臣秀吉の軍隊が朝鮮を侵略したとき、多くの陶工を連れて帰り、九州で産業を育成しようとしたからです。

3 Even though the Japanese invasion of Korea ended due to the death of Toyotomi Hideyoshi, this incident caused great troubles, both on the Korean Peninsula and for the Ming Dynasty.

豊臣秀吉の死によって日本の朝鮮侵略は終わりましたが、この事変は朝鮮半島と明朝に深刻なダメージを与えました。

6 関ヶ原の戦い

 こんな質問をされたら？

1 What caused the Battle of Sekigahara?

関ヶ原の戦いの原因はなんですか？

2 Who won the Battle of Sekigahara?

関ヶ原の戦いではだれが勝ちましたか？

3 How did government change as a result of the Battle of Sekigahara?

関ヶ原の戦いの結果、政治はどうなりましたか？

石田三成像

Battle of Sekigahara

💬 30秒で、こう答えよう！

1 After Toyotomi Hideyoshi's death, Tokugawa Ieyasu, one of the most powerful daimyo, and Ishida Mitsunari, Hideyoshi's senior attendant, struggled for power.

豊臣秀吉の死後、最も有力な大名の一人であった徳川家康と秀吉の側近であった石田三成が権力闘争を行ったことです。

2 The Battle of Sekigahara occurred in 1600, and Tokugawa Ieyasu and his allied daimyo defeated Ishida Mitsunari's army.

1600年、関ヶ原の戦いが起こり、徳川家康と彼と同盟した大名は石田三成の軍隊を敗りました。

3 After the Battle of Sekigahara, there was a drastic shift in power from the Toyotomi clan to the Tokugawa.

関ヶ原の戦い後、豊臣氏から徳川家へと劇的な権力の交代が行われました。

7 安土桃山文化

❓ こんな質問をされたら？

1 Why is it said that castles in this period became works of art?

この時代に城が芸術化したといいますが、どういうことですか？

2 Where can we find the influence of Western culture?

西洋文化の影響はどこに見ることができますか？

3 Who created the art of the tea ceremony?

茶道は誰によって確立されましたか？

千利休

Azuchi Momoyama culture

💬 30秒で、こう答えよう！

1 Powerful daimyo in the Azuchi Momoyama period erected castles with luxurious interiors. The artists of the Kano School created many *shoheki-ga* in famous castles during the Azuchi Momoyama period.

安土桃山時代の有力大名は内装が豪華な城を建立しまし、狩野派の絵師たちが有名な城で多くの障壁画を創作したからです。

2 The influence of *Nanban bunka*, or European culture, can be seen in the folding screens painted in the Azuchi Momoyama period.

南蛮文化の影響は安土桃山時代に描かれた屏風に見ることができます。

3 The tea ceremony was established by Sen no Rikyu, who came from Sakai, south of Osaka.

茶道は、大阪南部の堺出身である千利休によって確立されました。

第9章
Chapter 9

江戸時代

Edo Period

1 江戸時代の始まり

こんな質問をされたら？

1 When did the Edo period begin?
江戸時代はいつからいつまでですか？

2 Where was the *Edo Bakufu* located?
江戸幕府はどこにありましたか？

3 When did the Toyotomi administration end?
豊臣政権はいつ終わりましたか？

皇居

Beginning of the Edo Period

💬 30秒で、こう答えよう！

1. In 1603, Tokugawa Ieyasu was appointed shogun and established the Tokugawa Shogunate. The Edo period was between 1603 and 1868, and it was the era of the Tokugawa Shogunate.

   1603年、徳川家康は将軍に任命され、徳川幕府を開きました。江戸時代は1603年から1868年の間で、徳川幕府の時代でした。

2. In the Edo period, the shogun and his government were located in Edo Castle, the current Imperial Palace in Tokyo.

   江戸時代、将軍と幕府は江戸城におかれました。これは現在の東京にある皇居です。

3. It was 1615 when Tokugawa Ieyasu finally defeated Toyotomi Hideyori, the son of Toyotomi Hideyoshi, by attacking Osaka Castle.

   1615年に、徳川家康は大坂城を攻め立て、豊臣秀吉の子である豊臣秀頼をついに打ち負かしました。

第9章 江戸時代

2 徳川家康

❓ こんな質問をされたら？

1 What happened to Ieyasu when he was a child?

幼い頃の家康はどんなでしたか？

---

2 How did Ieyasu conquer the whole country?

家康はどうやって天下を取ったのですか？

---

3 How would you compare Nobunaga, Hideyoshi and Ieyasu?

信長、秀吉、家康をそれぞれ比較してください。

徳川家康

Tokugawa Ieyasu

💬 30秒で、こう答えよう！

1 When Tokugawa Ieyasu was a child, he lived as a hostage of the Imagawa, a strong clan in Suruga, the current Shizuoka Prefecture.

徳川家康は子どもの頃、現在の静岡県である駿河の有力大名である今川家の人質として過ごしました。

2 After Toyotomi Hideyoshi's death, Tokugawa Ieyasu defeated Ishida Mitsunari, his rival, and became the shogun in 1603.

豊臣秀吉の死後、徳川家康はライバルの石田三成を敗り、1603年、将軍になりました。

3 Tokugawa Ieyasu is called "the patient hero," while Toyotomi Hideyoshi is called "the manipulating hero," and Oda Nobunaga is known as "the radical hero."

徳川家康は「忍耐の英雄」と呼ばれます。一方、豊臣秀吉は「策略の英雄」と呼ばれ、織田信長は「革新的英雄」として知られています。

3 キリスト教の禁止

❓ こんな質問をされたら？

1 Why did the *Bakufu* ban Christianity?

幕府はなぜキリスト教を禁止したのですか？

2 When was Christianity banned?

キリスト教はいつ禁止されましたか？

3 What was the Shimabara Rebellion of Christians all about?

キリスト教徒の叛乱「島原の乱」とは？

踏み絵

天草四郎像

Banning Christianity

 30秒で、こう答えよう！

1 The Tokugawa Shogunate was concerned about the expansion of Christianity, fearing that Japan would be invaded by a Western power.

徳川幕府はキリスト教の普及を心配していました。日本が西洋の列強に侵略されるのでないかと恐れていたからです。

2 The Tokugawa Shogunate banned Christianity in 1612, and many Christians were martyred or deported from Japan.

徳川幕府は 1612 年、キリスト教を禁止しました。多くのキリスト教徒が迫害されたり、日本から追放されました。

3 In 1637, due to the heavy taxes and oppression of Christians, a large-scale revolt happened in the western part of Kyushu. More than 37,000 people came together to overthrow their local lords.

1637 年、重税とキリスト教徒への迫害のために、九州西部で大規模な反乱が起きました。3 万 7000 人以上が結束し、地域の大名を倒しました。

4 鎖国

❓ こんな質問をされたら？

1 When did the policy of national seclusion begin?

鎖国政策はいつ始まりましたか？

2 During the period of national seclusion, which countries did Japan trade with?

鎖国時代も交易していた外国はどこですか？

3 What was the impact of national seclusion policies?

鎖国政策による影響は？

鎖国時代の中国船

Closing of the Country

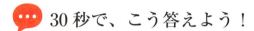 30秒で、こう答えよう！

1 After suppressing the Shimabara Revolt, the Tokugawa Shogunate decided to deport all the Spanish and Portuguese people from Japan.

島原の乱を鎮圧すると、徳川幕府はスペイン人とポルトガル人を日本から追放することに決めました。

2 After 1639, only Dutch, Chinese, and Koreans were allowed to maintain an international relationship with Japan. No Japanese people were allowed to leave or return to Japan.

1639年以降、オランダ、中国、朝鮮だけが日本と国際関係を維持することを許されていました。日本人の国外渡航は禁じられ、海外の日本人が日本に戻ることも禁じられました。

3 All the Japanese trading posts in Southeast Asia went into decline. The seclusion policy lasted more than 210 years and had a major influence on Japan's culture.

東南アジアのすべての日本の貿易拠点は衰退しました。鎖国政策は210年以上も続き、日本人の文化に大きな影響を与えました。

5 大名と幕府

❓ こんな質問をされたら？

1 What was the relationship between the daimyo and the *Bakufu*?

大名と幕府はどんな関係でしたか？

---

2 Which daimyo were the three branch families of the Tokugawa clan?

御三家とはどういう大名ですか？

---

3 What were the duties of the daimyo?

大名にはどんな義務がありましたか？

参勤交代行列図

Daimyo and the Bakufu

 30秒で、こう答えよう！

1 The shogunate controlled the feudal lords. Daimyo were feudal lords under the shogun, and they had the autonomy to govern their own domains.

> 幕府は大名を支配しました。大名とは将軍に臣ずる封建領主でしたが、領地を支配する自治権を持っていました。

2 *Go Sanke*, or the Great Three, were the three most important lords, and they were relatives of the shogun. They were the lords of Owari, Kii, and Mito.

> 御三家とは、最も重要な3大名家で、将軍の親族でした。彼らは、尾張、紀伊、水戸の大名でした。

3 Daimyo had to visit Edo every two years and stayed in Edo for one year to serve the shogun. The wives and sons of the daimyo had to live in Edo to prevent revolt by the daimyo.

> 大名は、2年ごとに江戸を訪れ、1年間江戸に留まり将軍に仕えなければなりませんでした。大名の妻子は、大名が謀反を起こさないように、江戸に住まなければなりませんでした。

6 身分制度と農本経済

❓ こんな質問をされたら？

1 What was the system of *shi-no-ko-sho*?

士農工商とはなんですか？

2 What was the annual *nengu*?

年貢とはなんですか？

3 How were the samurai paid?

侍の給料はどうなっていましたか？

農人（和漢三才図会）

Social Status and Economy Based on Agriculture

 30秒で、こう答えよう！

1 *Shi-no-ko-sho* was the class system enforced by the Tokugawa Shogunate, with the samurai at the top followed by the farmers, artisans, and merchants and it was strictly followed until the end of the Tokugawa era in 1868.

士農工商は徳川幕府によって施行された階級制度で、1868年に徳川時代が終わるまで、厳しく遵守させられました。頂点が侍で、農民、職人、商人がこれに続きました。

2 *Nengu* was the tribute or tax paid by farmers. The amount of a daimyo's wealth was calculated based on the amount of the domain's rice crop.

年貢とは、農民によって支払われる租税のことでした。大名の富の量は、領地の米の収穫高に基づいて計算されました。

3 In the Tokugawa era, the salary of samurai was paid in rice, and rice was converted into cash.

徳川時代、侍の給料は米で支払われ、その米を現金に替えていました。

7 元禄文化

❓ こんな質問をされたら？

1 What is the culture that was developed during the period of shogun Tsunayoshi called?

将軍綱吉の時代に発達した文化をなんといいますか？

---

2 What kinds of culture developed during the Genroku period?

元禄時代に発達した文化にはどのようなものがありますか？

---

3 What famous culture figures appeared during the Genroku period?

元禄時代の有名な文化人は誰ですか？

井原西鶴像
（生國魂神社）

Genroku Culture

💬 30秒で、こう答えよう！

1 Tokugawa Tsunayoshi was the fifth shogun of the Tokugawa Shogunate and his era, called *Genroku*, was the first peak of Edo and Kamigata culture.

徳川綱吉は第5代将軍でしたが、元禄という彼の治世は江戸と上方の文化が最初のピークを迎えました。

2 In the Genroku era, performing arts such as kabuki and bunraku became popular entertainment for the people of Edo and Osaka.

元禄時代、歌舞伎や文楽といった芸能は江戸や大阪の人たちに、娯楽として人気がありました。

3 Ihara Saikaku was a novelist and poet in the Genroku period, and his works such as *The Life of an Amorous Man* became big hits. Chikamatsu Monzaemon is known as the greatest dramatist in kabuki and bunraku theater.

井原西鶴は元禄時代の小説家であり俳人でしたが、『好色一代男』などの作品が大ヒットしました。近松門左衛門は歌舞伎や文楽の最も偉大な劇作家として知られています。

第9章 江戸時代

8 江戸時代の経済

? こんな質問をされたら？

1. What was the scale of Edo during that period?

   当時の江戸の規模はどのくらいですか？

2. What was transportation like during the Edo period?

   江戸時代の交通はどういうものでしたか？

3. During the Edo period, what was communication like?

   江戸時代の物流や情報通信はどうしていましたか？

飛脚

Economics of the Edo Period

 30秒で、こう答えよう！

1 In the eighteenth century, Edo became the biggest city in the world, and its population was over one million.

18世紀、江戸は世界一の大都市になりました。人口は100万人を超えていました。

---

2 The Edo Period was a very peaceful period so there was active exchange between the regions. Supporting this was the maintenance of the road system. Along each road, post towns with accommodations developed.

江戸時代は非常に平和な時代だったので、地域交流も活発になりました。それを支えたのが街道の整備です。また、各街道に宿場町が発達しました。

---

3 With the maintenance of the road system, a postal system was developed. A system of post-station relay couriers was created to speed up the communication of information.

街道の整備で郵便制度が発達し、飛脚と呼ばれる駅伝制度で情報の迅速化が図られました。

9 江戸時代の社会問題

❓ こんな質問をされたら？

1 What were the peasant uprisings?

一揆とはなんですか？

2 In what circumstances did the daimyo find themselves?

大名はどのような状況に置かれていましたか？

3 What was a major problem during the Edo period?

江戸時代の大きな社会問題はなんですか？

江戸時代の商人

Social Problems during the Edo Period

 30秒で、こう答えよう！

1 *Ikki* is a term that refers to farmers' revolts due to heavy taxes and poverty. Famine and poverty caused countless *ikki*, or farmers' revolts, in the late Edo period.

一揆とは、重い租税や貧困に対する農民の反乱を指すことばです。江戸時代の終わりには、飢饉と貧困は無数の一揆を引き起こしました。

2 Many daimyo were facing financial crises, and they had big debts to merchants incurred from running their *han*.

多くの大名が財政難に直面していました。藩を運営するために商人に巨額の負債を負っていました。

3 Large merchants appeared, accumulating enormous wealth, expanding the gap between the wealthy and the poor. A similar gap developed between the urban areas and agricultural villages.

大きな商人が出現し、富を蓄積していましたが、貧富の格差は拡大し、また都市と農村の格差も拡大しました。

10 化政文化

❓ こんな質問をされたら？

1 What kinds of ukiyo-e were there in this period?

この時代の浮世絵にはどういうものがありますか？

2 What was *Kokugaku*?

国学とはなんですか？

3 What was *Rangaku*?

蘭学とはなんですか？

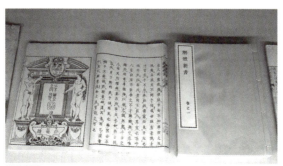

解体新書

Bunka Bunsei Culture

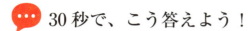 30秒で、こう答えよう！

1 Many famous ukiyo-e artists, such as Utamaro, Hokusai, Hiroshige, and Sharaku produced internationally famous works in the Bunka Bunsei period.

歌麿、北斎、広重、写楽といった多くの有名な浮世絵師たちが、文化文政時代に海外にもよく知られているような作品を描きました。

2 It's the study of the history and origin of the nation. Through the study of *kokugaku*, intellectuals considered that Japanese people must respect the emperor as divine.

国家の歴史や起源を研究することです。国学の研究により、知識層は日本人は天皇を神聖な存在として崇めるべきであると考えました。

3 *Rangaku* literally means "Dutch Learning," and it was the study of Western culture. Sugita Genpaku was a *rangaku* scholar who translated a Dutch medical book called the *Kaitai Shinsho*.

蘭学とは文字通りにいうと、「オランダ語の学習」を意味しますが、西洋文化を研究することでした。杉田玄白は蘭学者で、『解体新書』というオランダ語の医学書を翻訳しました。

11 開国

❓ こんな質問をされたら？

1 What was the situation like along the Japanese coast toward the end of the Edo period?

江戸後期の日本の沿岸はどんな状況でしたか？

2 Why did Japan give up national seclusion?

なぜ日本は鎖国をやめたのですか？

3 What were the results of opening the country?

開国の結果どうなりましたか？

マシュー・ペリー

Opening of the Country

💬 30 秒で、こう答えよう！

1 Starting around the end of the eighteenth century, many foreign ships appeared around Japan.

18 世紀末頃から、多くの外国船団が日本近海に現れました。

2 In 1853 and 1854, Commodore Perry and an American fleet appeared at Uraga, at the neck of Edo Bay. The appearance of the advanced steam ships shocked the Tokugawa Shogunate, and they decided to open the country.

1853 年と 1854 年に、ペリー提督とアメリカの艦隊が江戸湾の岬である浦賀に現れ、その進んだ蒸気船の登場は、徳川幕府に衝撃を与え、開国を決めました。

3 The *Nichibei Washin Joyaku* was signed in 1854, ending the seclusion policy. Many samurai and intellectuals were disappointed by the Tokugawa Shogunate's compromise, and they insisted on repelling the foreigners.

1854 年、日米和親条約が締結され、鎖国政策は終結しました。多くの侍や知識層は徳川幕府の妥協に失望し、外国人の排斥を主張しました。

第9章 江戸時代

12 尊王攘夷

❓ こんな質問をされたら？

1 What was the meaning of *sonno joi*?
尊王攘夷とはなんですか？

2 What kind of person was Yoshida Shoin?
吉田松陰とはどのような人物ですか？

3 What kind of person was Ii Naosuke?
井伊直弼とはどのような人物ですか？

吉田松陰

"Revere the Emperor and Expel the Foreigners"

 30秒で、こう答えよう！

1 *Sonno joi* was a concept and political slogan used around 1860. It means "Revere the emperor, expel the barbarians."

尊王攘夷とは、1860年頃に使われた概念であり、政治的なスローガンでした。天皇崇拝と外国人の排斥を意味します。

2 Yoshida Shoin was a scholar from Choshu, the current Yamaguchi Prefecture, who supported *sonno joi*. He was executed by Ii Naosuke. Many followers of Yoshida Shoin moved to Choshu to create a new order under the emperor.

吉田松陰は長州（現在の山口県）の学者で、尊王攘夷を支持しましたが、井伊直弼によって処刑されました。吉田松陰の多くの門弟たちは長州に移り、天皇の下に新しい秩序を創ろうとしました。

3 Ii Naosuke was the *tairo* of the Tokugawa Shogunate who tried to suppress the anti-foreigner movement. Ii Naosuke was assassinated by *ronin* from Mito in 1860.

井伊直弼は徳川幕府の大老で、外国人排斥運動を押さえようとしました。井伊直弼は、1860年水戸の浪人によって暗殺されました。

13 幕末の情勢

❓ こんな質問をされたら？

1 What kind of person was Katsu Kaishu?
勝海舟とはどういう人物ですか？

2 What kind of person was Sakamoto Ryoma?
坂本龍馬とはどういう人物ですか？

3 What was the *Shinsen-gumi*?
新撰組とはなんですか？

勝海舟

坂本龍馬

Conditions during Bakumatsu

 30秒で、こう答えよう！

1. Katsu Kaishu was a samurai of the Tokugawa Shogunate who was in charge of the navy and taught many of his followers to use Western technology. He founded the navy for the Shogunate.

   勝海舟は徳川幕府の侍で、海軍を指揮し、多くの弟子に西洋の技術を教えていました。また彼は幕府のために海軍を創設しました。

2. Sakamoto Ryoma was from Tosa, which is now Kochi Prefecture. He mediated between Satsuma and Choshu to help in the overthrow of the Tokugawa Shogunate.

   坂本龍馬は土佐（現在の高知県）出身でした。彼は薩摩と長州を仲介し、徳川幕府を覆すのに一役買いました。

3. The *Shinsen-gumi* were a special police force organized by the lord of Aizu to keep order in Kyoto, where *sonno joi* activists were very active.

   新撰組とは会津の大名によって組織された特別な治安部隊で、京都の秩序を守ろうとしました。当時の京都には、尊王攘夷の活動家が暗躍していました。

第9章 江戸時代

14 江戸幕府の滅亡

❓ こんな質問をされたら？

1 What was the thinking of the anti-*bakufu* clans centered on Satsuma and Choshu?

倒幕の中心、薩摩と長州はどういう考えでしたか？

---

2 How did the *bakufu* deal with Choshu?

幕府は長州にどう対応しましたか？

---

3 How did the *bakufu* come to an end?

江戸幕府の最後はどうなりましたか？

高杉晋作

徳川慶喜

Collapse of the Edo Bakufu

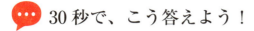 30 秒で、こう答えよう!

1. Both Choshu and Satsuma had conflicts with Western nations and recognized that repelling foreign power was impossible.

    長州と薩摩の両藩は西洋の国々と衝突したことがあり、海外の列強を駆逐することは不可能であると認識しました。

2. The Tokugawa Shogunate tried to defeat Choshu, but it failed. Takasugi Shinsaku led the troops of Choshu and repelled an attack by the Tokugawa Shogunate.

    徳川幕府は長州を打ち破ろうとしましたが、失敗に終わりました。高杉晋作は長州の軍隊を率いて、徳川幕府の攻撃を撃退しました。

3. In 1867, Tokugawa Yoshinobu, the fifteenth and last Shogun of the Tokugawa Shogunate, gave up his title and returned executive power to the imperial court. Katsu Kaishu negotiated with Saigo Takamori to surrender Edo Castle without a fight.

    1867 年、徳川幕府最後の将軍、第 15 代徳川慶喜は、その地位を降り、全権を朝廷に返しました。勝海舟は西郷隆盛と交渉し、江戸城を無血開城させました。

第10章
Chapter 10

明治時代

Meiji Period

明治維新

❓ こんな質問をされたら？

1　When did the Meiji Restoration occur?

明治維新は何年に起こりましたか？

2　What was the Boshin War?

戊辰戦争とはなんですか？

3　Who were the heroes of the Meiji Restoration?

明治維新の英雄は誰ですか？

西郷隆盛

木戸孝允

Meiji Restoration

💬 30秒で、こう答えよう！

1 The *Meiji Ishin*, or Meiji Restoration, was declared in 1868 by the imperial court, supported by Satsuma and Choshu.

明治維新は、薩摩と長州の支持を得た朝廷によって、1868年に宣言されました。

2 The Boshin War was a series of battles between pro-Tokugawa supporters and the new government. It ended in May of 1869 when Hakodate was seized by imperial troops.

戊辰戦争とは、徳川側と新政府側との間に起こった一連の戦いのことで、函館が朝廷側によって占拠された1869年5月に終結しました。

3 Kido Takayoshi of Choshu, Saigo Takamori, and Okubo Toshimichi from Satsuma were the three major figures who initiated the Meiji Restoration.

長州の木戸孝允、薩摩の西郷隆盛と大久保利通は明治維新を先導した三傑でした。

2 明治最初の政策

❓ こんな質問をされたら？

1 What happened to the Edo-period class system?

江戸時代の身分制度はどうなりましたか？

2 What happened to the samurai?

侍はどうなりましたか？

3 What happened in Edo and the provinces?

江戸や地方はどうなりましたか？

髷を落とし、洋装に改めた岩倉具視

Policies of the Early Meiji Period

 30秒で、こう答えよう！

1 Under the process of the Meiji Restoration, the feudal four-class system was abolished.

明治維新の過程で、封建的な4階級は廃止されました。

2 Under the direction of the Meiji government, samurai swords were prohibited, and people cut their samurai topknots, switching to Western hairstyles. The samurai disappeared from the Japanese system.

明治政府の指示により、侍の帯刀が禁止され、人々は髷を切って洋風の髪型に変えました。そして侍は日本の制度から姿を消しました。

3 In 1869, Edo was renamed Tokyo and became the nation's capital. *Han* were abolished and prefectures were set up in 1871.

1869年、江戸は東京に改名され、首都となりました。1871年、廃藩置県が行われました。

3 文明開化

❓ こんな質問をされたら？

1 When and where was Japan's first railroad built?

日本で最初の鉄道は、いつ、どこに、建設されましたか？

---

2 What was the policy of *fukoku kyohei*?

富国強兵とはなんですか？

---

3 What was the *shokusan kogyo*?

殖産興業とはなんですか？

日本の近代化に貢献した旧富岡製糸場（世界遺産）

Civilization and Enlightenment

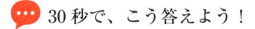 30秒で、こう答えよう！

1. Japan's first railroad service was begun in 1872 between Tokyo's Shinbashi and Yokohama.

   日本で最初の鉄道は1872年、東京の新橋と横浜間で運行されました。

2. *Fukoku kyohei* was a key slogan of the Meiji government. It means "Enrich the nation, strengthen the military."

   富国強兵は明治政府の主要なスローガンでした。「国を豊かにし、軍隊を強化する」ことを意味します。

3. *Shokusan kogyo* was another key slogan and vision of the Meiji government. It means "promotion of industry." The Meiji government invited many intellectuals and experts from abroad to Japan in order to create a strong, wealthy, industrialized nation.

   殖産興業は、明治政府のもう一つの主要なスローガンであり、ヴィジョンでもありました。これは「産業の促進」を意味します。明治政府は海外から多くの知識人と熟練工を日本へ招待し、強くて豊かな産業国を創ろうとしました。

第10章 明治時代

4 自由民権運動と憲法制定

❓ こんな質問をされたら？

1 Was there a movement for freedom in Japan?

日本では自由を求める運動はありましたか？

---

2 When was the cabinet system established and who was the first prime minister?

日本の内閣制度はいつでき、初代の総理大臣は誰ですか？

---

3 Under the constitution, what was the position of the Emperor?

憲法制定で天皇の地位はどうなりましたか？

伊藤博文

The Freedom and People's Rights Movement and Constitutional Assembly

 30秒で、こう答えよう！

1. The *Jiyu Minken Undo*, or Freedom and People's Rights Movement, spread after the Satsuma Rebellion.

   西南戦争後、自由民権運動が広がりました。

2. In 1885, the Meiji government implemented a cabinet system. Ito Hirobumi from Choshu became the first prime minister of Japan.

   1885年、明治政府は内閣制度を施行しました。長州出身の伊藤博文は日本で最初の総理大臣になりました。

3. Under the Meiji Constitution, the emperor was sovereign, and Japan was a monarchy in which the emperor was the supreme commander of the army and navy.

   明治憲法の下、天皇は最高権力者となり、日本は君主国となりました。天皇は、陸海軍の最高司令官となったのです。

5 日清戦争

❓ こんな質問をされたら？

1 How did the Sino-Japanese War, the first war following the restoration, occur?

明治以降最初の対外戦争である日清戦争はなぜ起こったのですか？

2 How did the Sino-Japanese War unfold?

日清戦争はどう展開しましたか？

3 What did Japan gain as a result of the Sino-Japanese War?

日清戦争の結果、日本は何を得ましたか？

日清戦争

Sino-Japanese War

💬 30秒で、こう答えよう！

1 Since Qing Dynasty China had a strong presence in Korea, Japanese people wanted to take Korea over from China. Thus, the Sino-Japanese war broke out.

中国の清朝は朝鮮に強い権益をもち、日本人はそれをくつがえそうとしました。このようにして、日清戦争は勃発しました。

2 The Sino-Japanese war ended in 1895 after Japan defeated the Qing army and navy thanks to the modernization that occurred during the Meiji Restoration.

日清戦争は1895年に終結し、日本が清の陸海軍を打ち破りました。これは、明治維新以来の近代化の賜物でした。

3 As a result of the Treaty of Shimonoseki, Japan gained Taiwan, the Penghu Islands, and financial compensation.

下関条約の結果、日本は台湾、澎湖諸島に加え賠償金を得ました。

6 日露戦争

❓ こんな質問をされたら？

1 Why did the Russo-Japanese War occur?

なぜ日露戦争は起こったのですか？

2 How did the Russo-Japanese War unfold?

日露戦争はどのように展開しましたか？

3 What did Japan gain as a result of the Russo-Japanese War?

日露戦争の結果、日本は何を得ましたか？

日露戦争　炎上するロシア艦

Russo-Japanese War

💬 30秒で、こう答えよう！

1 After the Sino-Japanese war, Japan confronted Russia over interests in northern China and the Korean Peninsula.

日清戦争後、日本は中国北部と朝鮮半島の利権を巡って、ロシアと衝突したのです。

2 For Japan, Russia seemed like too big a country to fight, but Japan defeated Russia in almost every battle.

日本にとって、ロシアは巨大すぎるくらいの国であり、戦うことなどできないように思われましたが、ほとんどすべての会戦で日本はロシアを破りました。

3 President Theodore Roosevelt arbitrated between Japan and Russia, and the Treaty of Portsmouth was signed in September of 1905. Japan took southern Manchuria and part of Sakhalin Island, but could not receive any financial compensation.

セオドア・ルーズベルト大統領が日本とロシアを仲裁し、1905年9月、ポーツマス条約が締結されました。日本は、南満州と樺太の一部を得ましたが、賠償金を受け取ることはできませんでした。

第10章 明治時代

7 明治時代の文化

❓ こんな質問をされたら？

1 What was *Bunmei Kaika*?

文明開化とは何ですか？

2 How did Japanese literature change in the Meiji period?

明治時代の日本の文学はどう変わりましたか？

3 How did Japanese artistic activity develop?

日本の芸術活動はどうなりましたか？

夏目漱石

Meiji Period Culture

 30秒で、こう答えよう！

1 *Bunmei kaika* means "civilization and enlightenment," and it was a popular expression among Japanese people to describe their rapid Westernization in the Meiji period.

文明開化とは「文明化と啓蒙」を意味し、明治時代の急速な西洋化を語るときに日本人が好んで使う表現でした。

2 Natsume Soseki was a novelist of the Meiji period and some of his works, such as *I am a Cat*, were translated into many languages.

夏目漱石は明治時代の小説家で、『吾輩は猫である』など幾つかの作品は多言語に翻訳されています。

3 In the Meiji period, Japanese traditional art was also exported to Europe. In particular, ukiyo-e influenced many Impressionists there.

明治時代、日本の伝統芸術もヨーロッパに輸出されました。特に浮世絵はヨーロッパの印象派に影響を与えました。

第11章
Chapter 11

大正時代

Taisho Period

大正時代の概要

❓ こんな質問をされたら？

1 When did the Meiji period end?

明治時代はいつ終わりましたか？

2 What were world affairs like during this period?

この時代の国際情勢はどうなっていましたか？

3 What were the political circumstances like in the Taisho period?

大正時代の政治状況はどのようなものでしたか？

大正天皇

Outline of the Taisho Period

💬 30秒で、こう答えよう！

1 Emperor Meiji died in 1912, bringing the turbulent 45-year era to an end. In 1912, Emperor Taisho succeeded to the throne.

明治天皇は1912年崩御し、騒然とした45年間が終わりました。同年に大正天皇が皇位を継承しました。

2 In 1914, two years after Emperor Taisho succeeded to the throne, the First World War broke out in Europe. During the First World War, Japan tried to expand its influence into China.

1914年、大正天皇が皇位を継承して2年後、ヨーロッパでは第一次世界大戦が勃発しました。第一次世界大戦で、日本は中国への影響力を拡大しようとしました。

3 Taisho Democracy was a widespread political movement in the Taisho era to make Japan a democratic nation.

大正デモクラシーとは大正時代の総合的な政治運動で、日本を民主主義国家にしました。

2 大正時代の政治

? こんな質問をされたら？

1 How was it that democracy progressed in the Taisho period?

大正時代に民主主義が進展したのは、どのような流れですか？

2 Was there a communist movement in Japan?

日本では共産主義運動がありましたか？

3 Was there a movement for improving the status of women?

日本では女性の地位向上運動はありましたか？

平塚雷鳥

Politics and Society in the Taisho Period

30秒で、こう答えよう！

1 Hara Takashi was the first prime minister whose cabinet was backed by public opinion. The cabinet of Kato Takaaki enacted The General Election Law, which granted all males over the age of 25 the right to vote.

原敬は民意に支持されて成立した最初の総理大臣です。加藤高明内閣は普通選挙法を施行し、25歳以上の全男子に選挙権が付与されました。

2 Due to the birth of the Soviet Union, Communism and the labor movement began to grow in Japan. The *Chian Iji Ho*, or the Peace Preservation Law, was enacted to crack down on Communism at the same time as the General Election Law was introduced.

ソビエト連邦の誕生により、日本で共産主義と労働運動が盛んになりました。治安維持法は普通選挙法と同じ頃施行され、共産主義を厳しく取り締まりました。

3 Yes, and Hiratsuka Raicho was one of the pioneers of the Japanese feminist movement.

はい。日本の女性解放運動の先駆けは、平塚雷鳥でした。

3 関東大震災

❓ こんな質問をされたら？

1 When did the Great Kanto Earthquake occur?
関東大震災はいつ起こりましたか？

2 What false rumors followed the earthquake?
関東大震災で起こったデマとは？

3 What impact did the earthquake have?
関東大震災からどんな影響がありなりましたか？

震災後の浅草寺周辺

The Great Kanto Earthquake

💬 30秒で、こう答えよう！

1 On September 1, 1923, Tokyo and its vicinity were struck by a magnitude 7.9 earthquake. The Great Kanto Earthquake resulted in over a hundred thousand deaths.

1923年9月1日、東京とその近郊はマグニチュード7.9の地震に襲われました。関東大震災によって、10万人以上の死者が出ました。

2 During the chaos after the earthquake, hundreds of Koreans were attacked and murdered by mobs due to rumors of possible riots by Koreans.

震災後の混沌の中で、朝鮮人による暴動が起きるという噂が流れ、多くの朝鮮人が虐殺されました。

3 The reconstruction after the Great Kanto Earthquake necessitated enormous government spending.

関東大震災の復興には、巨額の歳費を要しました。

4 大正時代の文化

❓ こんな質問をされたら？

1 When did broadcasting begin in Japan?

日本での放送の開始はいつですか？

2 What was the *Shirakaba* school in Japnese literature?

文学における白樺派とはなんですか？

3 Who was the most famous writer of the Taisho period?

大正時代の最も有名な作家は誰ですか？

芥川龍之介

Taisho Period Culture

💬 30秒で、こう答えよう！

1 In 1925, radio broadcasting services were started.

1925年、ラジオ放送が始まりました。

---

2 *Shirakaba-ha*, or the White Birch Group, was a group of authors who promoted the human spirit and a sense of freedom.

白樺派とは作家の集団で、人間の精神や自由な感覚を推奨しました。

---

3 Akutagawa Ryunosuke was known for his many highly literary short stories on classical subjects. His story *Rashomon* was later adopted as a film by Kurosawa Akira.

芥川龍之介は、古典的な題材についての文学性の高い多くの短編で知られていました。『羅生門』は後に黒澤明によって映画化されました。

第12章
Chapter 12

昭和──戦前
Showa Period: Prewar

1 大正から昭和へ

❓ こんな質問をされたら？

1 When did the Taisho period come to an end?
大正時代はいつ終わりましたか？

2 What kind of person was Emperor Showa?
昭和天皇とはどういう人物ですか？

3 What kind of period was the Showa period?
昭和とはどういう時代でしたか？

昭和天皇

From Taisho to Showa

 30秒で、こう答えよう！

1 Emperor Taisho passed away in 1926, and Emperor Showa succeeded to the throne.

1926年、大正天皇が崩御され、昭和天皇が皇位を継承しました。

2 Emperor Showa was a biologist who did research on marine organisms.

昭和天皇は、生物学者で海洋生物分類の研究者でもありました。

3 Prior to the war, during the period of militarism, civil freedom was greatly restricted, and Japan invaded China and Southeast Asia. Following the defeat, there was a complete change to a peaceful democratic society. By achieving unprecedented economic growth, Japan became the wealthiest country in the world.

戦前は軍国主義の時代で国民の自由も大きく制限され、中国や東南アジアへの侵略を行いました。敗戦後は一転自由で平和な民主主義社会になり、未曾有の経済成長を遂げ、世界でも最も豊かな国となりました。

2 世界恐慌

❓ こんな質問をされたら？

1 What influence did the global depression have on Japan?

世界恐慌は日本にも影響しましたか？

2 What happened to Japan's major enterprises due to the depression?

恐慌で日本の大企業はどうなりましたか？

3 What impact did this economic crisis have?

この経済危機はどのような影響を与えましたか？

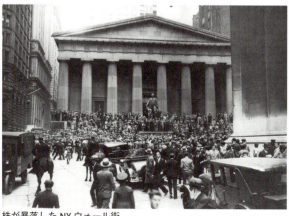

株が暴落したNYウォール街

Worldwide Panic

💬 30秒で、こう答えよう！

1　While the government struggled to recover from the financial damage of the Great Kanto Earthquake, the Great Depression occurred in the United States in 1929 and also hurt Japan.

政府が関東大震災の財政的損害から立ち直ろうともがいているとき、1929年アメリカで大恐慌が起こり、日本も被害を受けました。

2　*Zaibatsu*, the conglomerates such as Mitsui, Mitsubishi, and Sumitomo, became linked with politicians and tried to expand their own interests.

三井、三菱、住友のような財閥系の大企業は政治家と結びつき、自らの利権を拡大しようとしました。

3　In 1931, the Kwantung Army launched a military action and imposed military rule on Mukden. This was the infamous Mukden Incident.

1931年、関東軍は軍事行動を起こし、奉天を軍の支配下に置きました。これが悪名高い満州事変でした。

3 自由な社会の終焉

❓ こんな質問をされたら？

1 What was the early Showa period like?

昭和初期はどういう時代でしたか？

2 What happened in the 5.15 Incident?

5.15事件とはどのような事件ですか？

3 What happened in the 2.26 Incident?

2.26事件とはどのような事件ですか？

犬養 毅

Free Society Comes to an End

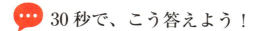 30秒で、こう答えよう！

1 Because of the continuing recession and consecutive international conflicts, radical nationalism spread in both the military and the general public.

終わりのない不景気と度重なる国際紛争のために、極端な国粋主義が軍部と一般大衆の中に広がりました。

2 On May 15, 1932, young naval officers conspired with army cadets to assassinate Prime Minister Inukai Tsuyoshi. The death of Inukai Tsuyoshi meant the end of the democratic government.

1932年5月15日、若い海軍将校が陸軍の士官候補生と共謀し、犬養毅首相を暗殺しました。犬養毅の死は、民主主義政府の終焉を意味しました。

3 On February 26, 1936, young army officers who wanted to stop social corruption and the power of the *zaibatsu* attempted a coup d'état, killing finance minister Takahashi Korekiyo and others.

1936年2月26日、若い陸軍将校たちは、社会の腐敗と財閥の専横に対してクーデターを起こし、高橋是清財務大臣などを暗殺しました。

4 日中戦争の開始

❓ こんな質問をされたら？

1 How did the Sino-Japanese War begin?

日中戦争はどのようにして起こりましたか？

2 How did the Chinese side respond?

中国側はどのような対応をしましたか？

3 What moves did the great Western powers make?

欧米列強はどう動きましたか？

蒋介石

Outbreak of the Sino-Japanese War

💬 30秒で、こう答えよう！

1 In July 1937, the Japanese army engaged in battle with the Chinese at Lugou Bridge on the outskirts of Beijing.

1937年7月、日本陸軍は北京郊外の盧溝橋で中国軍との戦争に入りました。

2 Jiang Jieshi unified the Chinese Nationalist Party and compromised with the Communist Party, and the nation as a whole held out against the Japanese.

蒋介石が国民党を統合し、さらに共産党とも妥協し、国家全体で日本と対峙することになりました。

3 To deal with Japanese expansion into Asia, the United States, Britain, China, and the Netherlands imposed an embargo on Japan.

日本のアジア侵攻に対処するために、米国、英国、中国、オランダは日本への禁輸措置を行いました。

第12章 昭和―戦前

5 日中戦争時の政策

❓ こんな質問をされたら？

1 During the Sino-Japanese War, how were Japanese citizen's lives affected by government policies?

日中戦争時、国民生活はどのような政策のもとにありましたか？

2 What was the situation in the National Diet?

国会はどういう状態でしたか？

3 What were international policies like?

対外的にはどういう政策でしたか？

ヒトラー

ムッソリーニ

Policies of the Sino-Japanese War

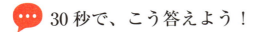 30秒で、こう答えよう！

1 In 1938, the National Mobilization Law was passed, granting the government unconditional powers to mobilize the people and national assets.

1938年、国家動員法が承認され、政府は国民と国家資産を無条件に統制運用できるようになりました。

2 In 1940, all political parties were brought under the Imperial Rule Assistance Association. This marked the end of party politics in Japan.

1940年、全政党は大政翼賛会のもとに統合されました。これにより、日本の政党政治は終焉しました。

3 The Japanese government announced the Greater East Asia Co-Prosperity Sphere and condemned the colonization of Asia by Western powers. Japan was controlled by the military and signed the Tripartite Pact with Italy and Germany.

日本政府は大東亜共栄圏を宣言し、欧米列強によるアジアの植民地化を非難しました。日本は陸軍に掌握され、イタリア、ドイツと三国同盟を結びました。

6 第二次世界大戦へ

❓ こんな質問をされたら？

1 When did World War II begin as far as Japan was concerned?

日本における第二次世界大戦はいつ始まりましたか？

2 Was there a conflict between the army and navy?

陸軍と海軍に対立があったのですか？

3 What was the situation like at the beginning of the war?

大戦初期の情勢はどうでしたか？

零戦

Toward World War II

💬 30秒で、こう答えよう！

1 On December 8, 1941, the Japanese navy attacked Pearl Harbor, and the Pacific War began.

1941年12月8日、日本海軍は真珠湾を攻撃し、太平洋戦争が始まりました。

2 The navy opposed going to war against the U.S. and the U.K. However, the navy was unable to stop the hardliners from the army.

海軍は米英に対する戦争には反対でした。しかし陸軍の強硬路線を止めることができませんでした。

3 At the beginning of the war, the Japanese army gained control over Singapore, Indonesia, and the Philippines. After its defeat in the Battle of Midway in June 1942, Japan was counterattacked by the Allies.

大戦初期に、日本陸軍はシンガポール、インドネシア、フィリピンを制圧しました。1942年6月、ミッドウェー海戦に敗れると、日本は連合軍に反撃されました。

7 敗戦に向けて

❓ こんな質問をされたら？

1 What happened to Japan's territory?
日本の国土はどうなりましたか？

2 What were the *kamikaze*?
神風とはなんですか？

3 When did Japan surrender?
日本はいつ降伏しましたか？

広島原爆ドーム

The Road to Defeat

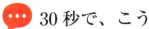 30秒で、こう答えよう！

1 Major cities all over Japan were exposed to bombings. On August 6 and 9, 1945, atomic bombs were dropped on Hiroshima and Nagasaki respectively.

日本中の大都市は爆撃に晒されました。1945年8月6日と9日、それぞれ広島と長崎に原爆が投下されました。

2 *Kamikaze* were suicide attacks by the Imperial Japanese Navy. Even human torpedoes were launched in the desperate battles against the Allies.

神風とは、日本海軍による自爆攻撃でした。連合軍との海戦では、人間魚雷さえも発射されました。

3 Japan surrendered on August 15, 1945, and the emperor informed the nation directly by radio broadcast. In Japan alone, there were more than three million casualties, and the country was devastated.

1945年8月15日、日本は降伏し、天皇はラジオで国民に直接それを伝えました。日本だけで、300万人以上の犠牲者を出し、国土は壊滅状態となりました。

第12章 昭和―戦前

第13章
Chapter 13

昭和──戦後
Showa Period: Postwar

1 日本の占領

❓ こんな質問をされたら？

1 What was GHQ and what did it do?

GHQ とはなんですか？

2 What was the International Military Tribunal for the Far East?

国際極東軍事裁判とはなんですか？

3 What happened to Japan's colonies?

日本の植民地はどうなりましたか？

昭和天皇とマッカーサー

Occupation of Japan

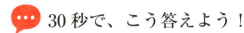

💬 30秒で、こう答えよう！

1 GHQ stands for General Headquarters, and it was where the Supreme Commander of the Allied Powers, Douglas MacArthur, worked to establish democracy in Japan.

GHQとは、総司令部のことで、そこでは連合国軍最高司令官であるダグラス・マッカーサーが日本に民主主義を確立するために着任しました。

2 The International Military Tribunal for the Far East was a series of trials to punish Class-A war criminals who were responsible for the wars in China and the Pacific.

国際極東軍事裁判とは、日中戦争や太平洋戦争で責任のあったA級戦犯を罰するために開かれた裁判のことです。

3 When Japan surrendered, Japan had to give up all its colonies, including Korea and Taiwan, and the lands Japan had taken over.

降伏したとき、日本は韓国と台湾を含むいままでに獲得した植民地を投げ出さねばなりませんでした。

2 日本の民主化

? こんな質問をされたら？

1 What happened to Japan's Constitution?

日本の憲法はどうなりましたか？

2 What happened to Japan's government?

日本の政治はどうなりましたか？

3 What happened to the Emperor?

天皇はどうなりましたか？

日本国憲法「上諭」

Democratization of Japan

 30秒で、こう答えよう！

1 On November 3, 1946, the Constitution of Japan was promulgated. Ever since, the Constitution of Japan has remained in force to the letter, with no amendments, as one of the world's fairest, most democratic constitutions.

1946年11月3日、日本国憲法が公布されました。公布されてから今まで、日本国憲法は世界で最も公平で民主的な憲法として、全く改正されることなく、一字一句効力を持ちつづけています。

2 Political parties were revived, and all men and women over twenty were given voting rights.

政党が復活し、20歳以上のすべての男女に選挙権が付与されました。

3 The emperor became the symbol of Japan, and Emperor Hirohito announced himself to be human rather than a divine being.

天皇は日本の象徴となり、昭和天皇は人間宣言を行いました。

3 冷戦と日本の主権回復

❓ こんな質問をされたら？

1 How did America's policies toward Japan change?

アメリカの対日政策はどう変化しましたか？

2 What happened to Japan's military?

日本の軍隊はどうなりましたか？

3 How did the return of Japanese sovereignty progress?

日本の主権回復はどう進みましたか？

サンフランシスコで署名する吉田茂

Cold War and the Return of Japanese Sovereignty

 30秒で、こう答えよう！

1 When the Cold War became serious, the United States changed its policy towards Japan and tried to convert Japan into a reliable ally in the Far East.

冷戦が深刻になると、米国は日本に対する政策を変え、日本を極東における信頼できる同盟国にしようとしました。

2 Based on the request of the United States, Japan re-armed and the Japan Self-Defense Force was created.

米国の要求に基づいて、日本は再軍備し、自衛隊が創設されました。

3 In 1951, 49 nations including America signed a peace treaty in San Francisco, and Japan became independent.

1951年、米国を含む49カ国がサンフランシスコで平和条約を締結し、日本は独立しました。

第13章 昭和—戦後

4 高度経済成長

❓ こんな質問をされたら？

1 What happened in Japan's postwar economy?

戦後日本の経済はどうなりましたか？

---

2 How did Japan's international policies change?

日本の対外政策はどうなりましたか？

---

3 What changes did Japanese economic development bring about?

日本の経済発展はどういう影響をもたらしましたか？

東京オリンピック 1964

Period of High Economic Growth

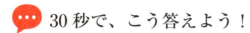 30秒で、こう答えよう！

1 In 1964, Japan hosted the Olympic Games and entered an era of dramatic economic growth called *kodo seicho*.

1964年、日本はオリンピックを開催し、高度成長といわれる劇的な経済成長の時代に入りました。

2 Under the Japan-US Security Treaty, Japan has cooperated with America as a member of the Western liberal nations. As a result, Japan has participated as a member of the summits of the Western developed nations and has enhanced its international standing.

日本は日米安保条約のもと、アメリカと協調して西側自由主義国の一員として発展しました。その結果、西側先進国によるサミットの一員となり、国際的地位は向上しました。

3 From the late 70s to the 80s, Japan became an economic superpower, and trade friction with the United States became a major international issue.

70年代終わりから80年代にかけて、日本は経済大国となり、アメリカとの貿易摩擦は大きな国際問題になりました。

第14章
Chapter 14

戦後から現代へ
Postwar Japan to the Present

日本文化の輸出

❓ こんな質問をされたら？

1 Who was a pioneer in introducing Japanese culture to the United States?

日本文化をアメリカに紹介した草分けは誰ですか？

---

2 Who was one of the first people to introduce Japanese literature abroad?

日本文学を最初に海外に紹介したのは誰ですか？

---

3 At present, what kind of Japanese culture can be found around the world?

現在、世界で市民権を得ている日本文化は何ですか？

エドワード・サイデンステッカー

Exporting Japanese Culture

💬 30秒で、こう答えよう!

1 It was Edwin O. Reischauer, a U.S. Ambassador to Japan, who had been knowledgeable about Japan since before the war and made a major contribution to formulating America's policy on Japan.

エドウィン・O・ライシャワーです。駐日大使でもあったライシャワーは、戦前からの知日派で、アメリカの対日政策の立案にも大きく貢献しました。

2 It was Edward Seidensticker, who translated Kawabata Yasunari's *Yukiguni* (*Snow Country*) and contributed to Kawabata being awarded the Nobel Prize for Literature.

エドワード・サイデンステッカーです。川端康成の『雪国』を翻訳し、川端のノーベル賞受賞に貢献しました。

3 The *otaku* culture of Japanese youth is organically spreading as it is adopted by young people in many countries and assimilated into their own lifestyle.

日本の若者のオタク文化は一つのまとまった文化として世界に広がり、海外の若者に率直に受け入れられ、彼らのライフスタイルの一部となっているようです。

2 憲法改正

❓ こんな質問をされたら？

1 What is the most controversial issue that Japan faces today?

いま、最も多くの議論が交わされている問題は何ですか？

2 What does Article 9 declare?

第9条は何を宣言していますか？

3 What do those who want to reform the Constitution stress?

改正派が主張しているのはどんなことですか？

ブルーインパルス

Revision of the Constitution

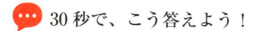 30秒で、こう答えよう！

1 It is whether to amend Article 9, the clause that renounces war.

戦争放棄条項である第9条を修正すべきかどうかという問題です。

2 This article declares that Japan cannot have armed forces and other war potential.

第9条は、日本が軍隊およびその他の戦力を持つことができないと宣言しています。

3 Those who want to revise this say that the nation should be allowed to set up a "National Defense Force."

改正派は、国家には「国防軍」の設置が認められるべきだと主張しています。

第14章 戦後から現代へ

3 靖国神社問題

❓ こんな質問をされたら？

1 What kind of shrine was Yasukuni Shrine in the beginning?

靖国神社はもともとどのような神社だったのですか？

2 What is the reason for the controversy at home and abroad?

国内外で軋轢の種となってきたのは何ですか？

3 What do China, South Korea and other Asian nations criticize?

中国や韓国などのアジア諸国は何を批判しているのですか？

靖国神社

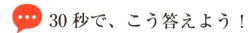
Yasukuni Shrine Issue

30秒で、こう答えよう！

1 As a memorial for Japan's war dead, Yasukuni Shrine was originally not so controversial.

靖国神社は、日本の戦死者の慰霊的な存在として、元来、そこまで物議を醸すようなことはなかったのです。

2 The shrine enshrines fourteen Class-A war criminals convicted at the Tokyo war crimes trials.

靖国神社が東京裁判で有罪判決を受けた14名のA級戦犯を祀っていることです。

3 They criticize Japan's Prime Minister's official visits as "a return to militarism" or "an incorrect interpretation of history."

彼らは日本の首相の公式参拝を「軍国主義への回帰」あるいは「誤った歴史解釈」であると批判しているのです

4 食料自給率

❓ こんな質問をされたら？

1 What is a nation's food self-sufficiency rate?

国の食料自給率とは何ですか？

2 How much has Japan's self-sufficiency rate decreased?

日本の食料自給率はどれほど下がってきているのですか？

3 What is the problem caused by a low food self-sufficiency rate?

食料自給率の低下は何が問題なのですか？

稲穂

Food Self-sufficiency Rate

 30秒で、こう答えよう！

1. It is the proportion of domestically produced food out of all the food that is consumed in that country.

    国内で消費されるすべての食料のうち、国内で生産された食料の割合のことです。

2. In 1965 Japan's food self-sufficiency rate stood at 73%. Since then, the rate has fallen, together with a trend of declining rice consumption. From the mid-1990s on, the self-sufficiency rate has remained at around 40%, dipping to 39% in the early 2010s.

    1965年の、日本の食料自給率は73％でした。以来、食料自給率は、米消費量の減少傾向とともに下降してきました。1990年代半ばからほぼ40％の横ばいで、2010年代初頭に39％に下がりました。

3. Food self-sufficiency affects national security. It makes Japan more dependent on other nations for its own survival.

    食料自給率は、国の安全保障をも左右するのです。日本は、他国に大きく依存して生きていかなければならなくなってしまうからです。

5 老舗(しにせ)

❓ こんな質問をされたら？

1 What are the characteristics of what is called a "long-established enterprise"?

老舗の特徴とは何ですか？

2 Is there something that symbolizes a long-established enterprise?

老舗のあかしみたいなものはあるのですか？

3 What kinds of shops are typical of this category?

典型的な老舗にはどのようなものがありますか？

暖簾

Shinise, Long-established Enterprises

 30秒で、こう答えよう！

1 Techniques, formulas, recipes and know-how accumulated over several generations go into products and services offered by *shinise*.

「老舗」が提供する商品やサービスには、数世代にわたり蓄積されてきた技術、製法、調理法、ノウハウが注ぎ込まれているのです。

2 This continuity of name and brand is often symbolized by the traditional curtain (*noren*) at the shop entrance.

店名や商標が代々続いているあかしは、店の入口に垂れ下がっている伝統的な布（暖簾）によく象徴されます。

3 The more typical shops are smaller, including sake makers and sellers of *wagashi* (Japanese-style confections), green tea, *tsukemono* (pickled vegetables), seasonings, and *tsukudani* (food boiled in soy source).

典型的な老舗は小規模で、日本酒の蔵元、和菓子やお茶、漬物、調味料、佃煮を売る店などがあります。

6 人口高齢化

❓ こんな質問をされたら？

1 What is the meaning of "aging society"?

「高齢化社会」とは何ですか？

2 How far has the graying of Japanese society advanced?

日本はいまどのように高齢化が進んでいるのですか？

3 What problems will occur as society continues to age?

このまま高齢化が進むとどんな問題が起きますか？

屋久杉

Graying of the Population

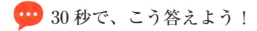 30秒で、こう答えよう!

1 *Koreika shakai*, an "aging society," is a society in which citizens aged 65 or older rise above 7% of the total population.

「高齢化社会」とは、65歳以上の国民が総人口の7%を超える社会のことです。

2 The average Japanese can expect to live close to two decades past retirement age, to age 83 for women and to 79 for men. As a result, it is estimated that by 2025 Japan will have the most top-heavy population pyramid in the world.

現在、日本人の平均寿命は、退職してから20年近く、女性は83歳、男性は79歳です。これが進むと、2025年には、日本は世界でもっとも逆三角形化の進んだ人口ピラミッドを抱えることになるでしょう。

3 The government will have to spend more money on pensions, housing, medical care and welfare programs for senior citizens.

国は、高齢者のための年金、住宅、医療および福祉制度に、より多くの予算を投入せねばならなくなります。

7 変わりゆく日本の男性像と女性像

❓ こんな質問をされたら？

1 What is an "herbivorous male"?

草食系男子とは何ですか？

---

2 What is a "carnivorous female"?

肉食系女子とは何ですか？

---

3 Why has the image of the Japanese male and female changed this much?

日本の男性像と女性像はなぜこのように変化してきたのですか？

「あなたも草食系？」